Amazingly Delicious
Bite-Size Treats

Cake Balls

Robin Ankeny and
Charlotte Lyon of

THE

Cake Ball®
COMPANY

Running Press
PHILADELPHIA · LONDON

© 2012 by Robin Ankeny and Charlotte Lyon
Photography © 2012 by Allan Penn

A Hollan Publishing, Inc. Concept
Published by Running Press,
A Member of the Perseus Books Group

Books published by Running Press are available at
special discounts for bulk purchases in the United
States by corporations, institutions, and other
organizations. For more information, please contact
the Special Markets Department at the Perseus
Books Group, 2300 Chestnut Street, Suite 200,
Philadelphia, PA 19103, or call (800) 810-4145, ext.
5000, or e-mail special.markets@perseusbooks.com.

ISBN 978-0-7624-4576-9
Library of Congress Control Number: 2011942351

E-book ISBN 978-0-7624-4690-2

9 8 7 6 5 4 3 2
Digit on the right indicates the number of this
printing

Cover design by Bill Jones
Edited by Jordana Tusman
Interior design by Amanda Richmond and
Trish Wilkinson
Typography: Samantha Upright, Minion Pro,
Duality, and Corbel

Running Press Book Publishers
2300 Chestnut Street
Philadelphia, PA 19103–4371

Visit us on the web!
www.runningpresscooks.com

For
Jackson, Luke, Morgan, and Elizabeth
whose sweetness inspires us daily

Contents

Why Cake Balls?

If you are new to the wonderful world of cake balls, then you might be asking yourself, "What the heck is a cake ball?" Well, let us tell you . . . they're just what you've been waiting for! They are crumbled bits of moist cake blended with rich icing, rolled into a ball, and then dipped in a deliciously wonderful chocolate coating. Cake balls are an exciting twist on the everyday cupcake and a sophisticated yet fun alternative to traditional dessert. It's no wonder why they've become such a sweet sensation!

Plain and simple, cake balls are pure greatness. There are a gazillion different variations of cake and icing, with every different flavor combination offering a unique, mouthwatering experience. And every bite delivers that thrilling combination we all love—cake and icing! Who hasn't been disappointed to realize that she has finished all the icing, leaving a sad slice of cake just begging for sticky sweet frosting? A cake ball promises to never leave your cake stranded.

The greatness doesn't just stop with the tastiness, either. Cake balls are just the right size. At The Cake Ball Company, we call them portion controlled. When you are feeling the need for something small and sweet, you can indulge without having to down a big slice of cake. Their ideal size also makes them perfect for parties and entertaining. You can set out your cake balls on a serving tray with napkins, and be done with it. There's no slicing, no plates, no forks, and no mess. Your guests can each have one cake ball, if they just want a little something sweet. Or, in the case of a recent party we hosted, a guest can stuff his face with ten! We won't name any names here, but you know who you are.

Maybe you are wondering how cake balls came to be. Maybe you aren't. But we'll tell you anyway. Robin grew up in a small southeast Texas town where her mother often served her one-of-a-kind cake balls at family events and celebrations. After Robin graduated from college, she moved to Dallas and brought her mother's cake ball recipe with her. She began making these cake balls for friends in the big city, where people had never heard of her tasty little treats before, and she started giving her unique cake balls as gifts. Gifts turned into favors, favors turned into requests, and, lo and behold, requests turned into orders. All the while, she experimented with new flavors.

Before she knew it, Robin had to go pro to keep up with the demand. Once out-of-town orders started coming in, Charlotte joined the operation. In 2006, the business officially became The Cake Ball Company, and we have worked every day since to make cake balls a part of the American everyday vocabulary. The Cake Ball Company now has a production facility and retail shop in Dallas. We hope that next time you find yourself in the Big D, you'll stop by the shop and say, "Howdy!" We have shipped cake balls to all fifty states, and we are constantly coming up with and testing new flavor combinations. In this tasty little cookbook, we've offered the most exciting and delicious recipes just for you.

We do work hard at The Cake Ball Company, but if there is one thing we know how to do best, it's have fun. The main philosophy of our business is, "Always have a ball." Laughing is the only way for us to remain sane when we are up to our elbows in hundreds of orders—and chocolate. Cake balls are not meant to be serious business. (How could it be when one is up to her elbows in chocolate?) So, we hope that you'll have a ball making the recipes in this cookbook. Experiment with the cake and icing combinations. Play with decorating ideas. Don't worry if they don't come out looking fabulous. By following our tips and tricks and with some practice, your balls can look just like the ones in this book. Don't forget that you can also order your cake balls from us at any time at www.cakeballs.com. We'll be happy to ship you a box of perfectly portion-controlled cake balls.

Getting Started

All right, it's time to get this ball rolling! We want to reiterate that the number one goal of this book is to get you to have fun with cake balls. Making cake balls is not rocket science; it's not even baking science, really. We want you to have a good time making the recipes, so don't take yourself too seriously—although it's pretty hard to when you've got your hands and face covered in cake and icing. If you have or know any rug rats, get them to help you with the recipes. Our kids have a blast experimenting with us in the kitchen. Or, try hosting a cake ball–making party with your friends. You'll enjoy sharing the experience with others, and the best part is that you all get to eat the end result.

We don't pretend to know everything there is to know about baking. We are not trained bakers with culinary degrees. Robin majored in parks and recreation and Charlotte majored in business. We just like to do it because it makes us happy. So, we tried to keep it simple for you because that is how we like to do our baking, too. With simplicity in mind, each recipe starts with one of three of our basic cake recipes: chocolate, vanilla, or yellow. And one of three basic icing recipes: chocolate, vanilla, or cream cheese. You can find these in the "Cake and Icing" section (page 29).

Now, since we are wives, mothers, and business owners with crazy, nutty schedules, we know that not everyone has the time or the wherewithal to bake a cake from scratch or get out the mixer and make some icing. So, we've adapted these recipes to work with store-bought cake mix and icing as well. Whichever you choose, from scratch or from the box, your cake balls will be fabulous!

Before you get rolling:

- Be sure to read through the entire recipe. Get out all the necessary ingredients and make sure you have enough of everything needed. We are a bit scatterbrained, so we don't always follow this, but trust us, you should!

- Set aside enough time to be successful with these recipes. Cake balls are not something you can make in fifteen minutes, even if you are using the cake mix versions. It is a good idea to bake, crumble, and roll your cake balls on day one. This part will require about two hours. You can then let them freeze overnight and dip and decorate the following day.

- Refer back to "Making Cake Balls" (page 17) for each recipe. Instead of including the same basic cake ball–making instructions with each recipe, we've included them once (page 17). These basic directions, tips, and techniques will hold true for every recipe in the book.

- You may notice that you don't need all of the icing you make (or open) for a particular cake ball recipe. Some people have asked what to do with the leftover icing. We would hate for the sugary goodness to go to waste, so try smearing icing between two cookies and having a cookie sandwich. You can also try spreading leftover icing on your morning scone or putting individual portions in shot glasses to serve at a party. That's a party we'd love to attend!

Equipment

Making great cake balls is not something you need super-special equipment for. But you will need a few basic baking tools to make your life easier as you make the recipes:

Cake Pan: We use 10-inch round aluminum cake pans that you can get at restaurant supply stores. They rock! Metal pans provide the most even heating and reliable results. You, of course, can use whatever you have on hand. Just be sure to adjust the baking time accordingly.

Cooking Spray: Spray your pans with cooking spray before you pour the cake batter in. It makes for easier cleanup. Cake balls can get messy, so take advantage of any extra help you can get!

Mixer: An electric mixer (stand or handheld) will make your life a lot easier, but a standard whisk will also do the trick.

Large Mixing Bowls: We use a big ol' mixing bowl to crumble the cake into and then incorporate the icing. A large bowl will give you room to really get your hands (or spatula) in there and blend the cake and icing together.

Electric Chopper or Mini Food Processor: An electric chopper is an awesome tool to have when making cake balls. We chop a lot of candy, cookies, fruit, nuts, and so on, and add them to our cakes to give them tons of flavor and texture. To get round balls, you'll need the ingredients to be finely chopped, and an electric chopper or processor is the best way to do that.

Cookie Scoopers: A small cookie scooper will help you portion your cake balls and keep them about the same size. You can also use a larger melon baller, small ice-cream scoop, or anything you can find to help you make even scoops.

Reusable Plastic Storage Containers: Storage containers are great for storing your rolled cake balls in the freezer before they are dipped. They are also great for keeping the finished product in the refrigerator until you are ready to indulge. You can also look for non-see-through ones to hide your precious cake balls from prying eyes.

Measuring Cups and Spoons: To measure with, silly.

Microwave: A microwave is the easiest way to melt your chocolate for dipping. You can melt small amounts at a time, making it easy to change from dark, milk, or white chocolate. A double boiler on the stove will also work if you prefer. See "Dipping and Drizzling" on page 20 for more information.

Microwave-Safe Glass Bowls: Small glass bowls are great for melting chocolate in the microwave. A deep one is best so you can easily dunk your cake ball into it. Glass bowls are best for melting choco-late because they won't overheat as do bowls made of ceramic, porcelain, or earthenware.

Paper Towels: It can get pretty messy while making cake balls. All that crumbling, mixing, and dipping requires some Brawny!

Toothpicks: We should really buy stock in toothpicks (if there is such a thing, let us know)! Every cake ball starts with a poke from a toothpick. It's the easiest way to shake off the excess chocolate and keep an even coating.

Teaspoons/Bar Spoons: Not a measuring teaspoon, but the long-handled kind that you stir your iced tea with. We use these to drizzle chocolate on our cake balls. It gives you easy control over where the drizzle is going.

Waxed Paper: After we dip our cake balls, we plop them on waxed paper while waiting to drizzle and decorate them. Waxed paper makes for easy cleanup, too. We should buy stock in waxed paper as well.

Patience and Creativity: We always say anyone can make a cake ball. It just takes a little patience, since it can be a bit time consuming. It also takes a bit of creativity when it comes to dipping and decorating. Tap in to your inner creative self, and have a good time!

Making Cake Balls

Professional-quality cake balls are relatively easy to create, if you follow these simple steps. We have attempted many different methods in making cake balls, but we keep coming back to these tried-and-true steps to create tasty and beautiful cake balls each and every time.

1. First, all cake balls must start with cake. So, the first step is to bake a cake. Follow the instructions for the cake recipe (pages 30–32).

2. After the cake has baked, remove it from the oven and slice it into four quarters. This will help it cool faster, and will give you sections to pick up for crumbling.

3. After the cake has cooled to room temperature, pick up each of the four sections and crumble it into a large mixing bowl using your hands. Continue to crumble the cake until you no longer see any chunks.

5. To create a consistent size for your cake balls, we recommend using a cookie scoop to portion out equal amounts of cake ball dough. We think a good size for a cake ball is about 1¼ inches in diameter. It is the perfect size to balance the ratio of cake to icing to chocolate coating. We like to scoop out all the portions before we start rolling.

6. Now you can start rolling. Take each portion that you've scooped

4. Next, you will combine the icing with the crumbled cake. Follow the instructions for making the icing (pages 33–34) and then add it to the bowl. The best way to mix it in is to just use a wooden spoon and some old-fashioned elbow grease. You will need to give the cake and icing mixture a good stir until it is fully combined and has a dough-like consistency.

out and roll it back and forth between your hands until you have a nice smooth ball. Place each ball on a tray lined with parchment or waxed paper.

7. After you have rolled all of the scooped-out portions, place the entire tray of balls in the freezer for at least 2 hours.

8. Before you take your cake balls out of the freezer, you'll need to prepare the dipping chocolate (page 20). Warm your chocolate using your preferred melting method.

9. Remove your cake balls from the freezer and spear each ball with a toothpick. Pick up a cake ball by the toothpick and dip it in the melted chocolate. Be sure to coat the entire ball. Then, lift the ball above the chocolate and give it a light shake to let the excess chocolate drip off. Set the dipped cake ball back down on the waxed paper

and move to the next cake ball. Continue to dip each cake ball until all of them are complete.

10. You'll now remove all the toothpicks and "cap." Using a spoon, take a small amount of the melted chocolate and cover the small holes where the toothpicks were.

11. You can now decorate the dipped cake balls according to the recipe or your imagination!

Dipping and Drizzling

Chocolate, oh chocolate, how we love you so. It is the most amazing food with the power to heal any ailments and make money grow on trees. Well, not really, but it sure does make people happy. That's why dipping your cake balls in sweet, sweet chocolate makes them that much more irresistible.

Dipping

There are many different types of chocolate you can use for dipping cake balls. Some people like to use almond bark or candy melts because it is a little easier to work with (and cheaper), but we prefer the taste of pure chocolate. The recipes in this cookbook call for you to dip the cake balls in dark, milk, and white chocolates. We have industrial vats of chocolate buttons in all three flavors at The Cake Ball Company. And they scream at us all day long to eat them. It is a hazard of being a CBC employee.

Anyway, you can use just about any brand of chocolate you like for dipping cake balls. If you visit a specialty food store, you can buy all types of chocolate formed in the shape of buttons. These are perfect for melting, and you can choose your preferred cocoa butter content. You can also use your favorite chocolate bars. If you are using bars, though, be sure to chop them up into equal-size pieces for even melting. Chocolate chips work fine as well.

For the at-home baker, we've found that melting chocolate in the microwave is a great way to get the job done. A microwave can melt the chocolate faster than a double boiler, with less effort and mess. If you do decide to melt your chocolate in a double boiler, just be sure not to get the water to a boiling point. The water should just be hot, so it doesn't scorch the chocolate.

To melt your chocolate in the microwave, start by filling a deep glass bowl with your chocolate buttons, chopped chocolate, or chocolate chips. For a single batch of cake balls, you'll need about 24 ounces of chocolate. You will want to use a glass bowl because it won't get too hot and burn the chocolate (or your hands). You can also use a large glass measuring cup. Make sure that whatever your glass bowl is, it is dry as a bone. Even a small drop of water can cause your chocolate to seize, which makes it thick and clumpy so your cake balls won't be smooth. Nobody wants cake balls with acne! You can also add 1 teaspoon of vegetable oil per 6 ounces of chocolate to help thin out your chocolate and make a nice sheen for your cake ball coating.

After you fill your bowl with the chocolate, place it in the microwave. It is difficult to give exact melting times as those greatly depend on the type and quantity of chocolate and the wattage of your microwave. A good place to start is by heating the chocolate for 90 seconds at 50 percent power. Take the bowl out and give it a good stir with a rubber spatula. Put it back in, and continue heating at 30-second to 1-minute intervals at 50 percent power. Continue to do this until only very small lumps of chocolate remain. Remove the bowl from the microwave and stir until the lumps are gone.

Once the chocolate is fully melted, allow it to sit at room temperature for about 1 minute, then you have to get to it! You'll need to dip and decorate fairly quickly, because the chocolate will set as it sits at room temperature. If you do take too long and the chocolate does firm up, no worries! Just follow the heating instructions again, being careful not to overheat the remaining chocolate.

Drizzling

You'll notice that many of our recipes call for you to drizzle the dipped cake balls with chocolate. The drizzle of chocolate helps add a decorative touch, but also helps the sprinkles, sugar crystals, or other garnishes stay in place. Friends often tell us that this part intimidates them. Once you do a few practice runs, you'll see there is nothing to be nervous about. We use a long teaspoon and dip it into our chocolate bowl to coat the very tip of the spoon with a bit of chocolate. It's usually enough to drizzle three to four cake balls at a time. Relax your shoulder and wrist and quickly move your hand back and forth to create a freeform zigzag pattern. It definitely gets easier with practice, and soon you'll be doing it with your eyes closed. Although, we wouldn't particularly recommend that.

Decorating

We think that decorating is the most fun part of making cake balls. This is your chance to get your creative juices flowing. There is really no end to all the fun things you can do with chocolate drizzles, sprin-

Quick Tips

- *Chop chocolate in equal-size pieces for even melting.*
- *Avoid getting any water in your chocolate.*
- *Use a glass bowl for microwave heating.*
- *Keep the heat low to avoid scorching.*
- *Continue to stir during melting.*
- *Work quickly after melting.*

kles, sanding sugar, nonpareils, and other ingredients. Visit your local craft store to see all the different kinds of sprinkles and other sweet decorations they offer.

At The Cake Ball Company, we prefer to use decoration that enhances the taste of the cake ball. You will notice that we often recommend using an ingredient from the recipe to finish off your cake balls. For example, we use chopped pistachios on top of the Chocolate Pistachio cake balls. The extra pistachios add more flavor and crunch to the overall experience. We have found that using candy colorings, sprays, and decorating gels can often add an unnatural taste. And, while we think that such things as candy melts, jelly beans, candy corn, and so on, can make your cake balls super cute, they can also make them taste kind of gross. At the end of the day, we prefer to eat our cake balls than to look at them, so we stick to decorations that make the cake balls taste great.

A good way to add a festive or distinctive decoration to your cake balls without affecting the taste is to attach a flag, tag, photo, or design to the toothpick that you used to dip your cake ball. This way you can customize your cake ball creations with something totally unique to you. Try cutting out the letters for something you want to say, such as "happy birthday" or "good luck." You can also buy letters already cut out at craft stores, in the scrapbooking sec-

tion. Attaching photos to the toothpicks can also make a super-cute idea for a birthday party, wedding, or baby shower. Be creative here. The possibilities are endless. If you can stick it to a toothpick, try it!

Tips and Troubleshooting

Everything you need to know to make beautiful and tasty cake balls is in this book. Chances are your first batch will not come out absolutely perfect, though. The first cake balls we made years ago came out a little lopsided and may have looked as though we dipped them with our toes. After making a few dozen, though, things got easier. It's just like Mom said: Practice makes perfect. Here is some advice to make your cake ball adventures easier:

- To avoid an icky, sticky mess, don't underbake your cake. Don't burn it, either, but it should be completely baked. If your cake is undercooked, you will get a sticky mess when you attempt to roll it into balls.

- On the same note, do not add too much icing to your cake crumbles. As you go through the recipes in this book, you will find that adding ingredients to the basic cake recipes will change the volume and consistency of the finished product. If you are using our icing recipes, you may need to adjust the amounts used to get the perfect dough-like consistency. Start by adding ¼ can or ¼ cup and then add more as needed. Refrigerating the dough for 30 minutes to 1 hour before rolling will also help prevent things from getting too sticky.

- When combining the cake crumbles and icing, get your hands in the bowl and really incorporate the two. Use this as an opportunity to get out some aggression. Knead it, punch it, and really mash it all together. We use extra large mixing bowls, so we can really get in there.

- Don't try to dip your cake balls too soon after they are rolled. Make sure they have had at least 2 hours to firm up in the freezer. The chocolate does not adhere as well to a warm cake ball. Also, the toothpick will hold better in a cold cake ball.

- Don't overheat your chocolate. Follow the instructions on page 21 for melting chocolate carefully.

- When a recipe calls for added nuts, fruits, or candy, these should be chopped up in a food processer or electric chopper. Large pieces of ingredients will make for a lumpy and bumpy ball. We prefer our cake balls to be round and smooth.

- Cake balls freeze well. You can keep them in an airtight container in the freezer for a few months, if you can control yourself not to eat them first. They will also keep in the refrigerator for a week or so. We recommend storing the finished cake balls in the refrigerator. We also prefer to eat our cake balls with a slight chill to them, so we serve them straight from the fridge. Some people do prefer them at room temperature, though. It really is a personal preference depending on what you like!

- Each recipe will yield between 40 and 55 balls, but it really depends on you, the cake ball maker. It depends on the scooper that you use, how much icing you use, how well incorporated your dough is, the ingredients added to the cake, and how much of the baked cake you snack on before you start incorporating the icing. You'll get a better idea of quantity the more times you make cake balls.

Parties, Displays, and Gift-Giving

You certainly don't need a particular reason to make cake balls, but some ideas include baby and bridal showers, sports game parties, holiday parties, birthday parties, kids' parties, or just about any reason people may gather together.

Cake balls really are the perfect party treat. They are bite-size, require no extraneous utensils, and everyone loves them.

We've found that displaying cake balls on tiered serving trays makes for a nice presentation at a party. You can also just use regular serving trays placed on books or boxes to add varying height. Some home decor stores sell specialized serving

pieces made for mini cupcakes that also work nicely for cake balls.

You may have seen cake balls served on lollipop sticks. This is a cute display idea. You can stick the ends of the lollipop sticks into a Styrofoam block, and present them this way at an event. Your guests can just grab their balls by the stick!

Cake balls are great to serve at events, but they also make unique and thoughtful gift ideas. Certain craft and container stores sell endless amounts of cute gift containers. There are paper, wooden, metal,

plastic, round, square, tall, skinny, or fat ones. They come in all different colors and shapes, so surely one is bound to fit your gift-giving needs. Package a few cake balls in a cute container and attach a sweet note. Bam! You are that person's new favorite friend. Easy as pie (or cake balls)!

We have sold quite a few cake balls as wedding favors in our time. They really are the perfect sweet treat to end a beautiful wedding day. You can create fantastic favors by putting a cake ball or two in a cellophane bag and tying with a pretty ribbon to match your colors. You can also put a

easy breezy! And, just recently, we had a soon-to-be mom come in to the shop and give us a sealed envelope from her doctor that contained the sex of her baby. She asked us to open the envelope and then make either strawberry or blueberry cake balls, dipped and decorated in a generic way. After dinner, she and her friends and family all bit into their cake balls at the same time to see if she was having a boy or girl. Surprise! Pink strawberry cake balls meant she was having a girl. What a sweet memory for the baby book!

couple of cake balls in a small box and affix a monogrammed sticker to personalize your treats. Some other wedding ideas that we've done include cake balls in place of a traditional wedding cake, or displayed on a dessert buffet. They can also be passed out on trays with milk or coffee as a late-night snack as the reception is winding down.

Babies are big for cake balls, too. They don't eat them, but their parents, friends, and family sure do to celebrate their arrival! We have many customers that pick up a box of cake balls to take to the hospital to visit new babies. Again, they are just so easy to serve and eat. Cake balls work great at baby showers for the same reason:

CAKE
AND ICING

All of the cake ball recipes in this book are based on the following basic cake and icing recipes. If you don't have time or energy to make cake or icing from scratch, you can start with a box cake mix or store-bought icing. It's completely up to you.

Cake

Basic Chocolate Cake

2 cups all-purpose flour

¾ cup unsweetened cocoa
powder

2 teaspoons baking soda

½ teaspoon salt

2 teaspoons vinegar

1 cup milk

2 cups granulated sugar

2 eggs, at room temperature

½ cup vegetable oil

2 teaspoons vanilla extract

1. Preheat the oven to 350°F and grease a 10-inch round cake pan.

2. In a medium-size bowl, combine the flour, cocoa, baking soda, and salt with a wire whisk and set aside. In a separate small bowl or cup, stir the vinegar into the milk.

3. In a large bowl, use an electric mixer to blend together the sugar, eggs, vegetable oil, 1 cup of water, and the milk mixture. Add the vanilla and blend until completely combined. Slowly add the dry mixture to the wet mixture until fully combined.

4. Pour the batter into the cake pan and bake for 30 to 40 minutes, or until fully baked. Let cool.

Basic Vanilla Cake

1. Preheat the oven to 350°F and grease a 10-inch round cake pan.

2. With an electric mixer, cream together the sugar and butter. Beat in the eggs and vanilla.

3. In a separate bowl, mix together the flour and baking powder, and then add to the wet mixture. Stir in the milk.

4. Pour the batter into the cake pan and bake for 30 to 40 minutes, or until fully baked. Let cool.

1 cup granulated sugar

4 ounces (1 stick) unsalted butter, softened

2 eggs, at room temperature

1 tablespoon vanilla extract

1½ cups all-purpose flour

1¾ teaspoons baking powder

½ cup milk

Basic Yellow Cake

2 cups all-purpose flour

2 teaspoons baking powder

½ teaspoon salt

4 ounces (1 stick) unsalted butter, softened

1 cup granulated sugar

3 large eggs, at room temperature

2 teaspoons vanilla extract

¾ cup milk

1. Preheat the oven to 350°F and grease a 10-inch round cake pan.

2. In a medium-size bowl, combine the flour, baking powder, and salt with a wire whisk and set aside.

3. In a large bowl, use an electric mixer to cream the butter and sugar until light and fluffy. Beat in the eggs, one at a time. Add the vanilla and mix until completely combined.

4. Slowly alternate between adding the flour mixture and the milk to the wet mixture, mixing until smooth.

5. Pour the batter into the cake pan and bake for 30 to 40 minutes, or until fully baked. Let cool.

Icing

Basic Chocolate Icing

4 tablespoons unsalted butter

¼ cup plus 2 tablespoons cocoa powder

1 (16-ounce) package confectioners' sugar

¼ cup plus 3 tablespoons milk, warm

1 teaspoon vanilla extract

Use an electric mixer on medium speed to cream the butter. Add the cocoa and mix well. Slowly beat in the sugar, adding the warm milk until smooth. Stir in the vanilla.

Basic Vanilla Icing

2 cups confectioners' sugar

2 tablespoons unsalted butter, softened

2 tablespoons milk

½ teaspoon vanilla extract

With an electric mixer on medium speed, combine all the ingredients in a bowl and beat until smooth and fluffy.

Basic Cream Cheese Icing

4 tablespoons unsalted butter, softened
4 ounces cream cheese, softened
1 teaspoon vanilla extract
1¼ cups confectioners' sugar

With an electric mixer on medium speed, beat together the butter and cream cheese until smooth. Mix in the vanilla. Slowly mix in the sugar until smooth and creamy.

CLASSICS

The Cake Ball Company opened its doors in 2006 with six decadent flavors. Today, those first six flavors are fondly referred to as our classics. These include Birthday Cake, which is our most popular, Chocolate Toffee, German Chocolate, Brownie, Southern Red Velvet, and Wedding Cake. Although we have had a blast trying and testing new flavors, these six remain the best sellers in our shop and on our website. The Cake Ball Company has been steadily rolling uphill since our modest beginnings with these tried-and-true flavors.

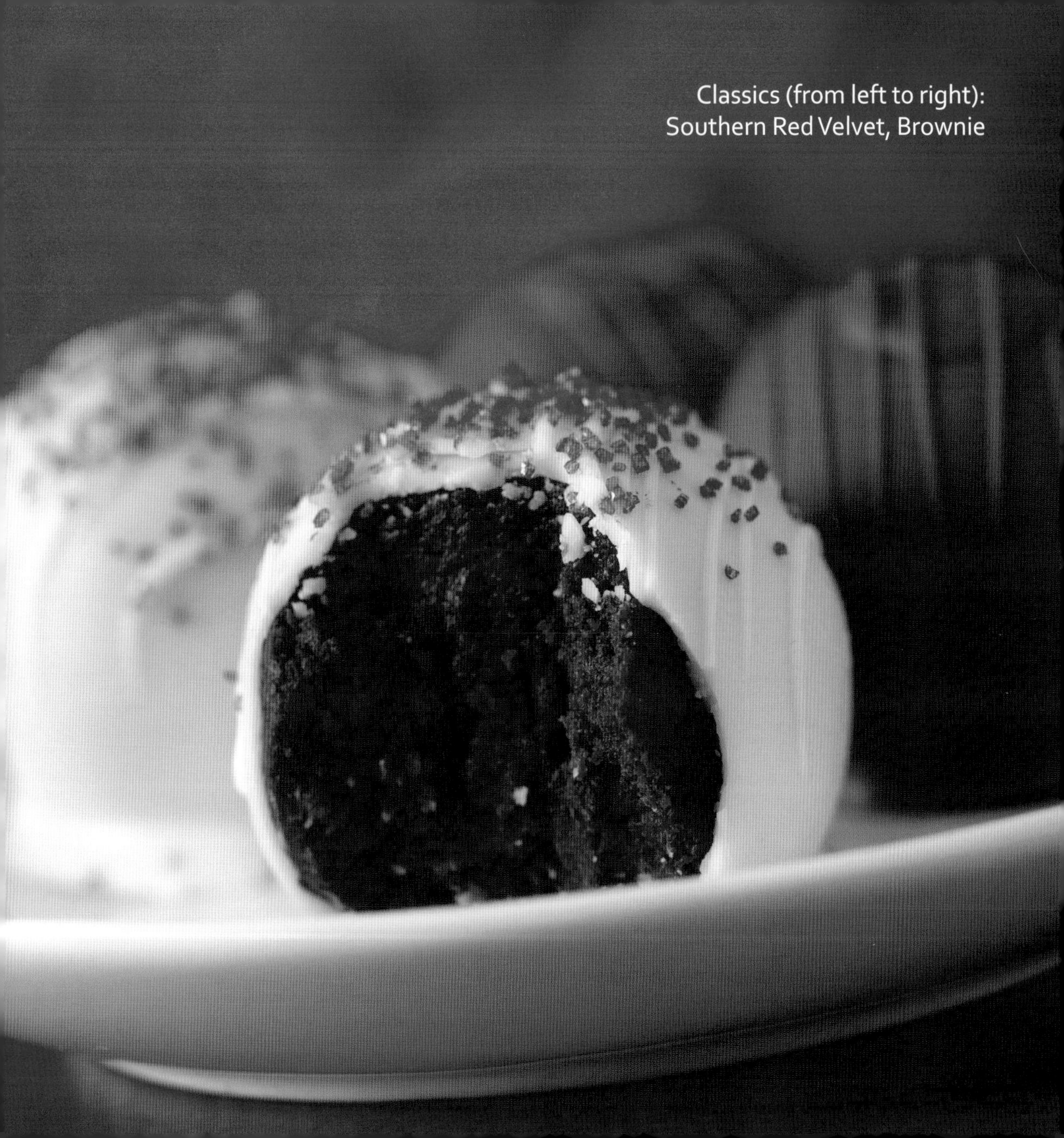

Classics (from left to right):
Southern Red Velvet, Brownie

Birthday Cake

This is the recipe for the first cake ball ever sold and remains our most popular flavor to date. It is the most basic of all recipes, but makes a great blank canvas to add flavors to, flex your creative muscles, or experiment with some fun decorating ideas.

1. Follow the instructions for baking a vanilla cake (page 31).

2. While the cake is cooling, prepare the cream cheese icing (page 34) or open your store-bought icing.

3. After the cake has cooled, follow the cake ball method instructions (page 17).

4. After the cake balls are dipped in white chocolate, drizzle them with fine lines. Do one at a time and sprinkle with rainbow sprinkles to give each a festive feel.

FOR THE CAKE AND ICING:

1 (18.25-ounce) box vanilla cake mix or basic vanilla cake (page 31)

½ to ¾ cup basic cream cheese icing (page 34) or store-bought cream cheese icing

FOR COATING AND DECORATING:

24 ounces white chocolate, for coating

About ½ cup rainbow sprinkles, for decoration

Chocolate Toffee

The addition of toffee to a cake ball makes for a yummy, crunchy surprise. This was one of our original flavors and is still a best seller to this day. Try adding more toffee bits, if you really like a good crunch!

FOR THE CAKE AND ICING:

1 (18.25-ounce) box vanilla cake mix or basic vanilla cake (page 31)

½ to ¾ cup basic cream cheese icing (page 34) or store-bought cream cheese icing

1 cup English toffee bits

FOR COATING AND DECORATING:

24 ounces milk chocolate, for coating

About ½ cup English toffee bits, for decoration

1. Follow the instructions for baking a vanilla cake (page 31).

2. While the cake is cooling, prepare the cream cheese icing (page 34) or open your store-bought icing.

3. After the cake has completely cooled, follow the cake ball method instructions (page 17). As you are incorporating the icing with the crumbled cake, add the toffee bits.

4. After the cake balls are dipped in milk chocolate, drizzle them with fine lines. Do one at a time and sprinkle with the toffee bits to add more crunchy toffee flavor.

German Chocolate

Now we know this is not how your grandmother used to make a German chocolate cake, but your grandmother probably didn't make cake balls, either. Once you mash up all the ingredients in a bowl, you'll find this tastes just as yummy as (if not better than) hers!

1. Mix together the ingredients for making a chocolate cake (page 30). After the ingredients are fully combined, stir in the coconut, pecans, and sundae syrup.

2. Follow the instructions for baking the cake (page 30).

3. While the cake is cooling, prepare the chocolate icing (page 33) or open your store-bought icing. Note that this recipe calls for less icing than normal because the cake is already super moist from the sundae syrup.

4. After the cake has cooled, follow the cake ball method instructions (page 17).

5. After the cake balls are dipped in milk chocolate, place a piece of shaved coconut in the cap. Sprinkle with a little sugar.

Quick Tip: *If you really like your coconut and pecans, try adding more of both when you incorporate the icing.*

FOR THE CAKE AND ICING:

1 (18.25-ounce) box chocolate cake mix or basic chocolate cake (page 30)

1½ cups sweetened flaked coconut

1 cup finely chopped pecans

1 cup caramel sundae syrup

½ cup basic chocolate icing (page 33) or store-bought chocolate icing

FOR COATING AND DECORATING:

24 ounces milk chocolate, for coating

About ½ cup sweetened shaved coconut, for garnish

Granulated sugar, for garnish

Brownie

This is our second-best-selling cake ball. It is pretty simple, but a big hit every time.
It tastes like fudgy brownies. If you aren't a fan of pecans (we love 'em),
you can try another nut or omit the nuts altogether.

FOR THE CAKE AND ICING:

1 (18.25-ounce) box chocolate
cake mix or basic chocolate
cake (page 30)

½ cup finely chopped pecans

½ to ¾ cup basic chocolate
icing (page 33) or store-
bought chocolate icing

FOR COATING AND DECORATING:

24 ounces milk chocolate,
for coating

1. Mix together the ingredients for making a chocolate cake (page 30). After the ingredients are fully combined, stir in the pecans.

2. Follow the instructions for baking the cake (page 30).

3. While the cake is cooling, prepare the chocolate icing (page 33) or open your store-bought icing.

4. After the cake has cooled, follow the cake ball method instructions (page 17).

5. After the cake balls are dipped in milk chocolate, drizzle them with fine lines. Or you can let your imagination run wild! This flavor makes a great blank canvas to try out some fun decorating ideas.

Southern Red Velvet

Sometimes we joke about changing the name of our company to the Red Velvet Cake Ball Company because this is one of our most requested flavors. Honestly, these are not our favorite cake balls to make because, well, they are red and messy! Robin wants to make a Not-So-Red Velvet Cake Ball where we leave out the dye, but that just seems un-American.

1. Mix together the ingredients for making a chocolate cake (page 30). After the ingredients are fully combined, stir in the cocoa and red food coloring.

2. Follow the instructions for baking the cake (page 30).

3. While the cake is cooling, prepare the cream cheese icing (page 34) or open your store-bought icing.

4. After the cake has cooled, follow the cake ball method instructions (page 17).

5. After the cake balls are dipped in white chocolate, drizzle them with fine lines. Do one at a time and sprinkle with the red sprinkles.

FOR THE CAKE AND ICING:

1 (18.25-ounce) box chocolate cake mix or basic chocolate cake (page 30)

2 tablespoons unsweetened cocoa powder

1 (1-ounce) bottle red food coloring

½ to ¾ cup basic cream cheese icing (page 34) or store-bought cream cheese icing

FOR COATING AND DECORATING:

24 ounces white chocolate, for coating

About ½ cup red sprinkles, for decoration

Wedding Cake

We love weddings, and this cake ball is our tribute to a perfect wedding day. While there's nothing quite like a traditional wedding cake, we've found that serving cake balls can be a bit more exciting and unique. The addition of coconut and pecans in our vanilla cake gives a nod to the typical Italian cream cake so often served. Say "I do" to wedding cake balls!

FOR THE CAKE AND ICING:

1 (18.25-ounce) box vanilla cake mix or basic vanilla cake (page 31)

1 cup sweetened flaked coconut

½ cup finely chopped pecans

½ to ¾ cup basic cream cheese icing (page 34) or store-bought cream cheese icing

FOR COATING AND DECORATING:

24 ounces white chocolate, for coating

About ¼ cup clear sprinkles, for decoration

1. Mix together the ingredients for making a vanilla cake (page 31). After the ingredients are fully combined, stir in the coconut and pecans.

2. Follow the instructions for baking the cake (page 31).

3. While the cake is cooling, prepare the icing (page 34) or open your store-bought icing.

4. After the cake has cooled, follow the cake ball method instructions (page 17).

5. We like to keep these simple and elegant. After the cake balls are dipped in white chocolate, drizzle them with fine lines. Do one at a time and sprinkle with clear sprinkles to give each a shimmering sparkle.

CHOCOLATE
LOVERS

Everything goes better with chocolate, right? It certainly holds true with chocolate cake balls, anyway. The ingredients we were working with and incorporating into our chocolate cakes were sometimes hard not to indulge in here and there: candy bars, butterscotch, chocolate-covered pretzels, and chocolate-covered coffee beans, to name a few. More than once, we had to run back to the store to pick up more chocolaty ingredients. We strongly believe the old adage to be true: a day without chocolate is like a day without sunshine!

Chocolate Lovers (from left to right):
Chocolate Macadamia, Chocolate Butterscotch,
Chocolate Coffee Hazelnut

Candy Bar Overload

It seems that everyone loves Snickers bars. So, to create our Candy Bar Overload Cake Ball, we added crushed Snickers bars to our favorite chocolate cake and icing. The combo of one of the world's most famous candy bars along with decadent cake and icing dipped in milk chocolate is simply Snickerific!

1. Follow the instructions for baking a chocolate cake (page 30).

2. While the cake is cooling, prepare the icing (page 33) or open your store-bought icing.

3. After the cake has cooled, follow the cake ball method instructions (page 17). Add the chopped Snickers to the crumbled cake and icing and incorporate well.

4. After the cake balls are dipped in milk chocolate, place a piece of chopped Snickers bar in the milk chocolate cap.

Quick Tip: *If Snickers isn't your favorite candy bar, omit the Snickers and replace with a fun candy bar alternative.*

FOR THE CAKE AND ICING:

1 (18.25-ounce) box chocolate cake mix or basic chocolate cake (page 30)

½ to ¾ cup basic chocolate icing (page 33) or store-bought chocolate icing

2 cups chopped Snickers bars (2 to 3 bars)

FOR COATING AND DECORATING:

24 ounces milk chocolate, for coating

About ½ cup coarsely chopped Snickers bars, for decoration (1 to 2 bars)

Chocolate Buzz

This cake ball is a definite favorite among chocoholics, which we proudly call ourselves! The "buzz" comes from the small amount of coffee in it, and helps bring out the chocolate and cinnamon flavors. If you like more coffee flavor, feel free to add more granules.

FOR THE CAKE AND ICING:

1 (18.25-ounce) box chocolate cake mix or basic chocolate cake (page 30)

1 tablespoon instant coffee granules

1 teaspoon ground cinnamon

½ to ¾ cup basic chocolate icing (page 33) or store-bought chocolate icing

FOR COATING AND DECORATING:

24 ounces dark chocolate, for coating

1 tablespoon ground cinnamon, for garnish

1. Mix together the ingredients for making a chocolate cake (page 30). After the ingredients are fully combined, stir in the instant coffee granules and cinnamon.

2. Follow the instructions for baking the cake (page 30).

3. While the cake is cooling, prepare the chocolate icing (page 33) or open your store-bought icing.

4. After the cake has cooled, follow the cake ball method instructions (page 17).

5. After the cake balls are dipped in dark chocolate, drizzle them with fine lines. Do one at a time and sprinkle with the ground cinnamon.

Chocolate-Covered Cherry

The partnership between chocolate and cherries is tried-and-true. So why not put them together in cake ball form? You'll find that the result is incredibly delectable! The cherry pie filling adds body and moistness, so you won't need as much icing when making these.

1. Mix together the ingredients for making a chocolate cake (page 30). After the ingredients are fully combined, stir in the cherry pie filling. Use your electric mixer to crush the cherries a little into the batter.

2. Follow the instructions for baking the cake (page 30).

3. While the cake is cooling, prepare the icing (page 33) or open your store-bought icing. You will use less icing for this cake ball than normal because the cake is already super moist from the pie filling.

4. After the cake has cooled, follow the cake ball method instructions (page 17).

5. After the cake balls are dipped in dark chocolate, place a piece of dried cherry in the dark chocolate cap.

FOR THE CAKE AND ICING:

1 (18.25-ounce) box chocolate cake mix or basic chocolate cake (page 30)

1 (12.5-ounce) can cherry pie filling

½ to ¾ cup basic chocolate icing (page 33) or store-bought chocolate icing

FOR COATING AND DECORATING:

24 ounces dark chocolate, for coating

About ½ cup dried cherries, cut into small pieces, for garnish

Chocolate Butterscotch

*The inspiration for this flavor came from a friend's dessert she calls "sex in a pan."
It is traditionally made by poking holes in a chocolate sheet cake and
pouring butterscotch sundae topping, Cool Whip, and nuts on top. Try our
cake ball version, and see if you are left saying, "Oh, my!"*

FOR THE CAKE AND ICING:

1 (18.25-ounce) box chocolate cake mix or basic chocolate cake (page 30)

1 (12.25-ounce) jar butterscotch sundae syrup

½ cup finely chopped pecans

½ cup basic chocolate icing (page 33) or store-bought chocolate icing

1 (11-ounce) bag butterscotch hard candies, finely chopped

FOR COATING AND DECORATING:

24 ounces milk chocolate, for coating

About 55 butterscotch hard candies, crushed, for garnish

1. Mix together the ingredients for making a chocolate cake (page 30). After the ingredients are fully combined, stir in the butterscotch sundae syrup and pecans.

2. Follow the instructions for baking the cake (page 30).

3. While the cake is cooling, prepare the icing (page 33) or open your store-bought icing. Note that this recipe calls for less icing than normal because the cake is already super moist from the sundae syrup.

4. After the cake has cooled, follow the cake ball method instructions (page 17). Add the butterscotch candy to the cake crumbles and icing. Be sure to remove any large pieces of candy.

5. After the cake balls are dipped in milk chocolate, drizzle them with fine lines. Sprinkle them with the crushed butterscotch pieces.

Chocolate Coffee Hazelnut

Hazelnuts are one of our favorite nuts to use in our cake balls because they are sweet and buttery. And hazelnuts pair nicely with vanilla and other common baking flavors, such as coffee and chocolate. This rich, fudgy cake ball combines all of these incredible flavors and makes for one deliciously nutty ball.

1. Mix together the ingredients for making a chocolate cake (page 30). Stir in the instant coffee granules.

2. Follow the instructions for baking the cake (page 30).

3. While the cake is cooling, prepare the icing (page 33) or open your store-bought icing.

4. After the cake has cooled, follow the cake ball method instructions (page 17). Add the chopped hazelnuts to the cake crumbles and icing. Adding the hazelnuts at this point gives the dough a nice crunchy texture. Be sure to remove any large pieces of hazelnut.

5. After the cake balls are dipped in milk chocolate, drizzle them with the chocolate and top each with a whole hazelnut piece.

Quick Tip: *If you are a coffeeholic, feel free to add more coffee granules for more coffee flavor. You can also try decorating with a chocolate-dipped espresso bean.*

FOR THE CAKE AND ICING:

1 (18.25-ounce) box chocolate cake mix or basic chocolate cake (page 30)

4 teaspoons instant coffee granules

½ cup chopped hazelnuts

½ to ¾ cup basic chocolate icing (page 33) or store-bought chocolate icing

FOR COATING AND DECORATING:

24 ounces milk chocolate, for coating

About 55 whole hazelnuts, for garnish

Chocolate Salty Pretzel

At The Cake Ball Company, we love salty and sweet combos. The Chocolate Salty Pretzel Cake Ball is the perfect mix of rich chocolate and crunchy, salty pretzels. We used white chocolate–covered pretzels in our version to add another bit of the wow factor, but you can use any type of pretzel you want. You can even add toffee bits for more buttery and crunchy goodness.

FOR THE CAKE AND ICING:

1 (18.25-ounce) box chocolate cake mix or basic chocolate cake (page 30)

1 (6-ounce) package white chocolate–covered pretzels, crushed, divided

½ to ¾ cup basic chocolate icing (page 33) or store-bought chocolate icing

FOR COATING AND DECORATING:

24 ounces milk chocolate, for coating

About ½ cup roughly crushed pretzel pieces, for garnish

1. Mix together the ingredients for making a chocolate cake (page 30). After the ingredients are fully combined, stir in half of the crushed pretzels, about ¾ cup.

2. Follow the instructions for baking the cake (page 30).

3. While the cake is cooling, prepare the icing (page 33) or open your store-bought icing.

4. After the cake has cooled, follow the cake ball method instructions (page 17) and add the other half of the crushed pretzels to the cake crumbles and icing.

5. After the cake balls are dipped in milk chocolate, drizzle them with the chocolate and sprinkle with the crushed pretzel pieces. Or you can try decorating with a whole chocolate-dipped pretzel for a fun alternative.

Chocolate Macadamia

Here is another chocolate and nutty combination that makes for a tasty cake ball with lots of flavor and texture. The addition of the pears and cinnamon add a special surprise to your average chocolate cake. The first million-dollar winner of the Pillsbury Bake-Off contest inspired this recipe. Once you make this cake ball, you will see what all of the buzz was about!

FOR THE CAKE AND ICING:

1 (18.25-ounce) box chocolate cake mix or basic chocolate cake (page 30)

1 cup finely chopped macadamia nuts

1 (6-ounce) can pears in light syrup, drained and pulverized

1 teaspoon ground cinnamon

½ to ¾ cup basic chocolate icing (page 33) or store-bought chocolate icing

1. Mix together the ingredients for making a chocolate cake (page 30). After the ingredients are fully combined, stir in ½ cup of the chopped macadamia nuts, blended pears, and cinnamon.

2. Follow the instructions for baking the cake (page 30).

3. While the cake is cooling, prepare the icing (page 33) or open your store-bought icing.

4. After the cake has cooled, follow the cake ball method instructions (page 17). Add the additional ½ cup of chopped macadamia nuts to the cake crumbles and icing. Be sure to remove any large pieces of macadamia.

5. After the cake balls are dipped in dark chocolate, drizzle them with the chocolate and top with the chopped macadamia nuts.

FOR COATING AND DECORATING:

24 ounces dark chocolate, for coating

About ½ cup chopped macadamia nuts, for garnish

Chocolate Pistachio

We like to snack on the funny little nuts known as pistachios.
So, one day we thought: let's put them in a cake ball. And, lo and behold,
they taste even better when combined with chocolate. Imagine that!

1. Mix together the ingredients for making a chocolate cake (page 30). Stir in the pistachio pudding. After the ingredients are fully combined, stir in ½ cup of the pistachios.

2. Follow the instructions for baking the cake (page 30).

3. While the cake is cooling, prepare the icing (page 33) or open your store-bought icing.

4. After the cake has cooled, follow the cake ball method instructions (page 17). Add the additional ½ cup of chopped pistachios to the cake crumbles and icing. Be sure to remove any large pieces of pistachio.

5. After the cake balls are dipped in milk chocolate, drizzle them with the chocolate and top each with a pistachio piece.

FOR THE CAKE AND ICING:

1 (18.25-ounce) box chocolate cake mix or basic chocolate cake (page 30)

1 (3.4-ounce) package instant pistachio pudding

1 cup finely chopped pistachios, divided

½ to ¾ cup basic chocolate icing (page 33) or store-bought chocolate icing

FOR COATING AND DECORATING:

24 ounces milk chocolate, for coating

About ½ cup whole pistachios, for garnish

Triple Chocolate Chip

Dark chocolate, milk chocolate, and white chocolate chips combine in a chocolaty cake to create a triple threat of chocolaty goodness! This cake ball is sure to wow all the chocoholics in your life.

FOR THE CAKE AND ICING:

1 (18.25-ounce) box chocolate cake mix or basic chocolate cake (page 30)

½ cup dark chocolate chips

½ cup milk chocolate chips

½ cup white chocolate chips

½ to ¾ cup basic chocolate icing (page 33) or store-bought chocolate icing

FOR COATING AND DECORATING:

24 ounces dark chocolate, for coating

About ½ cup chocolate shavings, for garnish

1. Mix together the ingredients for making a chocolate cake (page 30). After the ingredients are fully combined, stir in the chocolate chips.

2. Follow the instructions for baking the cake (page 30).

3. While the cake is cooling, prepare the icing (page 33) or open your store-bought icing.

4. After the cake has cooled, follow the cake ball method instructions (page 17).

5. After the cake balls are dipped in dark chocolate, drizzle them with the chocolate and top with the chocolate shavings. Get creative with your decorations and place the shavings vertically to create a piece of chocolate cake ball art.

Quick Tip: *If you really love your chocolate chips as Charlotte does, then add more of each when you are incorporating your icing with the cake.*

FRESH AND FRUITY

Part of your commitment to healthy eating means having your recommended daily fruit—but commitment to having your daily fruity cake ball is equally (if not more!) important. This chapter is one of the longest because there are just so many tasty fruits to enjoy. The cake balls in this chapter are perfect for your next brunch or lunch. Move over, muffins, the fruity cake ball has arrived! It's time to start baking and rolling your way to happier days.

Fresh and Fruity: Banana Walnut, Blackberry Cobbler, Lemon

Apple Cinnamon

One thing that we love about apples is that they just go so great with cinnamon.
This may seem like more cinnamon than you'd normally use in a cake,
but after you incorporate the icing, you'll see that it is just the right amount.

FOR THE CAKE AND ICING:

1 (18.25-ounce) box yellow cake mix or basic yellow cake (page 32)

3 Granny Smith apples, peeled, cored, and shredded (about 2½ cups)

3 teaspoons ground cinnamon

½ cup finely chopped walnuts

½ to ¾ cup basic cream cheese icing (page 34) or store-bought cream cheese icing

FOR COATING AND DECORATING:

24 ounces white chocolate, for coating

About ½ cup dried apples, cut into small pieces, for garnish

About 1 tablespoon ground cinnamon, for garnish

1. Mix together the ingredients for making a yellow cake (page 32). After the ingredients are fully combined, stir in the shredded apple, cinnamon, and chopped walnuts.

2. Follow the instructions for baking the cake (page 32).

3. While the cake is cooling, prepare the icing (page 34) or open your store-bought icing.

4. After the cake has cooled, follow the cake ball method instructions (page 17).

5. After the cake balls are dipped in white chocolate, place a piece of dried apple in the white chocolate cap. Sprinkle with the cinnamon.

Quick Tip: *Try giving these as teacher gifts or serve them at your next picnic. They say an apple a day keeps the doctor away, but we have a feeling your doctor may just love a box of these Apple Cinnamon cake balls as a treat on your next visit.*

Banana Walnut

When we started The Cake Ball Company back in 2006, we came up with the idea for Brunch Balls. Banana Walnut was our first attempt at a Brunch Ball, and proved to be a sweet success. Try serving these at your next brunch affair or keep them in your freezer to enjoy in the morning for breakfast. The sweet taste of banana chunks paired with the walnuts and chocolate will have you grabbing one (or two!) each morning on your way out the door.

FOR THE CAKE AND ICING:

1 (18.25-ounce) box yellow cake mix or basic yellow cake (page 32)

3 ripe medium bananas, mashed (about 2½ cups)

¾ cup finely chopped walnuts

½ to ¾ cup basic cream cheese icing (page 34) or store-bought cream cheese icing

FOR COATING AND DECORATING:

24 ounces white chocolate, for coating

About ½ cup walnut pieces, for garnish

1. Mix together the ingredients for making a yellow cake (page 32). After the ingredients are fully combined, stir in the bananas and walnuts.

2. Follow the instructions for baking the cake (page 32).

3. While the cake is cooling, prepare the icing (page 34) or open your store-bought icing.

4. After the cake has cooled, follow the cake ball method instructions (page 17).

5. After the cake balls are dipped in white chocolate, place a walnut piece in the white chocolate cap.

Orange Poppy Seed

This cake ball has an incredible summer flavor. The orange is refreshing and the poppy seeds add a surprising textural pop. This is a bit of an old-fashioned recipe that makes the perfect cake ball for a lazy summer afternoon.

1. Mix together the ingredients for making a vanilla cake, substituting the orange juice for the water, if using the box version, or for the milk, if making the cake from scratch (page 31). After the ingredients are fully combined, stir in the poppy seeds and the orange zest.

2. Follow the instructions for baking the cake (page 31).

3. While the cake is cooling, prepare the icing (page 33) or open your store-bought icing.

4. After the cake has cooled, follow the cake ball method instructions (page 17).

5. After the cake balls are dipped in white chocolate, place a candied orange peel in the cap.

Quick Tip: Topping these with candied orange peel makes for an elegant presentation. You can buy candied peel in specialty food shops or online. If you are up to it, you can also make your own. Look online for a quick and easy recipe.

FOR THE CAKE AND ICING:

1 (18.25-ounce) box vanilla cake mix or basic vanilla cake (page 31)

1 cup orange juice

2½ tablespoons poppy seeds

Zest from 2 large oranges

½ to ¾ cup basic vanilla icing (page 33) or store-bought vanilla icing

FOR COATING AND DECORATING:

24 ounces white chocolate, for coating

About 55 candied orange peels, for garnish

Blueberry Muffin

The aroma of fresh blueberries baking in the vanilla cake will make you oh so anxious to get started on rolling these cake balls. When your cake is combined with the vanilla icing and dunked in white chocolate, we guarantee you will never look at a muffin the same way again.

1. Mix together the ingredients for making a vanilla cake (page 31). After the ingredients are fully combined, fold in the blueberries.

2. Follow the instructions for baking the cake (page 31).

3. While the cake is cooling, prepare the icing (page 33) or open your store-bought icing.

4. After the cake has cooled, follow the cake ball method instructions (page 17).

5. After the cake balls are dipped in white chocolate, place a blueberry in the white chocolate cap. Garnish with the blue sprinkles.

Quick Tip: If you are up to it, make a streusel or crumb topping to sprinkle on top instead of the blue sprinkles. An easy topping can be made from 1 cup of light brown sugar, 1 cup of flour, and ¼ cup of diced butter. Mix it all together until crumbly and bake in the oven at 350°F for 10 minutes.

FOR THE CAKE AND ICING:

1 (18.25-ounce) box vanilla cake mix or basic vanilla cake (page 31)

1 (6-ounce) package fresh blueberries

½ to ¾ cup basic vanilla icing (page 33) or store-bought vanilla icing

FOR COATING AND DECORATING:

24 ounces white chocolate, for coating

About 55 blueberries, for garnish

About ¼ cup blue sprinkles, for decoration

Chocolate Apricot

We think everything goes great with chocolate, and in the fruit world, this is true for apricots especially. The addition of crystallized ginger in this recipe makes for a special spicy surprise. Combine the ginger with chunks of dried apricots, and you get a perfect texture that makes for a whole lot of tasty treasures.

FOR THE CAKE AND ICING:

1 (18.25-ounce) box chocolate cake mix or basic chocolate cake (page 30)

1 (7-ounce) package dried apricots, chopped

⅔ cup crystallized ginger, ground finely

½ to ¾ cup basic chocolate icing (page 33) or store-bought chocolate icing

FOR COATING AND DECORATING:

24 ounces milk chocolate, for coating

About 55 dried apricots, for garnish

1. Mix together the ingredients for making a chocolate cake (page 30). After the ingredients are fully combined, stir in the apricots and ginger.

2. Follow the instructions for baking the cake (page 30).

3. While the cake is cooling, prepare the icing (page 33) or open your store-bought icing.

4. After the cake has cooled, follow the cake ball method instructions (page 17).

5. After the cake balls are dipped in milk chocolate, place an apricot in the milk chocolate cap.

Quick Tip: Use an electric chopper or mini food processor to grind up the crystallized ginger and dried apricots.

Blackberry Cobbler

Blackberries are known as the cabernet of berries. We like any berry that can be compared to a wine. So, we love blackberries, and when added to this cake with the spices, we think you will, too! June and July are perfect months to make these cake balls because blackberries are in season then and will be refreshingly plump and juicy.

FOR THE CAKE AND ICING:

1 (18.25-ounce) box yellow cake mix or basic yellow cake (page 32)

1 teaspoon freshly grated nutmeg

1 teaspoon ground cinnamon

½ teaspoon ground allspice

½ teaspoon ground cloves

1 (6-ounce) package fresh blackberries, roughly chopped

½ to ¾ cup basic vanilla icing (page 33) or store-bought vanilla icing

1. Mix together the ingredients for making a yellow cake (page 32). After the ingredients are fully combined, stir in the nutmeg, cinnamon, allspice, and cloves. Then fold in the blackberries.

2. Follow the instructions for baking the cake (page 32).

3. While the cake is cooling, prepare the icing (page 33) or open your store-bought icing.

4. After the cake has cooled, follow the cake ball method instructions (page 17).

5. After the cake balls are dipped in white chocolate, place a blackberry in the white chocolate cap.

Quick Tip: *Buy some extra blackberries at your local farmers' market during blackberry season and freeze them for use in later months.*

FOR COATING AND DECORATING:

24 ounces white chocolate, for coating

About 55 blackberries, for garnish

Coconut Cream

We love coconut. Pacific Islanders refer to the coconut tree as the tree of life.
I think we'd agree. Unfortunately, they don't grow so well in Dallas. Oh well! We'll survive
by eating coconut in our cake. Coconut definitely takes center stage in this cake ball,
as coconut milk and flaked coconut shine in a charming vanilla cake and icing combo.

1. Mix together the ingredients for making a vanilla cake, substituting the coconut milk for the water, if using the box version, or for the milk, if making the cake from scratch (page 31). After the ingredients are fully combined, stir in the flaked coconut.

2. Follow the instructions for baking the cake (page 31).

3. While the cake is cooling, prepare the icing (page 33) or open your store-bought icing.

4. After the cake has cooled, follow the cake ball method instructions (page 17).

5. After the cake balls are dipped in milk chocolate, drizzle them with fine lines. Sprinkle with the flaked coconut.

Quick Tip: For a delicious and chewy alternative, try topping these with chopped Mounds bars instead of the flaked coconut. Mmmmounds.

FOR THE CAKE AND ICING:

1 (18.25-ounce) box vanilla cake mix or basic vanilla cake (page 31)

1 (13.5-ounce) can coconut milk

1½ cups sweetened flaked coconut

½ to ¾ cup basic vanilla icing (page 33) or store-bought vanilla icing

FOR COATING AND DECORATING:

24 ounces milk chocolate, for coating

About ½ cup sweetened flaked coconut, for garnish

Strawberries and Cream

Even those who claim not to like fruit always like strawberries! It may very well be the perfect fruit. At least our kids think so. They eat strawberries like they are going out of style. This recipe was created for them by Robin's sweet mother. The addition of the strawberry jam adds an especially sweet strawberry flavor—and proves that Mom always know best!

FOR THE CAKE AND ICING:

1 (18.25-ounce) box vanilla cake mix or basic vanilla cake (page 31)

¼ cup strawberry-flavored gelatin

¼ cup seedless strawberry jam

½ to ¾ cup basic cream cheese icing (page 34) or store-bought cream cheese icing

FOR COATING AND DECORATING:

24 ounces milk chocolate, for coating

About ½ cup melted white chocolate, for decoration

About ½ cup sliced strawberries, for garnish

1. Mix together the ingredients for making a vanilla cake (page 31). After the ingredients are fully combined, stir in the strawberry gelatin and strawberry jam.

2. Follow the instructions for baking the cake (page 31).

3. While the cake is cooling, prepare the icing (page 34) or open your store-bought icing.

4. After the cake has cooled, follow the cake ball method instructions (page 17).

5. After the cake balls are dipped in milk chocolate, drizzle them with the melted white chocolate, then place a sliced strawberry in the cap.

Hummingbird

This is Charlotte's "most favoritest cake in the whole wide world." Despite the name, you won't find a single hummingbird listed in the ingredients. You will, however, find bananas, pineapple, pecans, and cinnamon, and boy, do they taste fantastic together! It is a decadent Southern specialty, which makes for an unbelievable cake ball.

FOR THE CAKE AND ICING:

- 1 (18.25-ounce) box vanilla cake mix or basic vanilla cake (page 31)
- 1 teaspoon ground cinnamon
- 2 ripe medium bananas, mashed (about 1 cup)
- 1 (8-ounce) can crushed pineapple, drained
- 1 cup finely chopped pecans
- ½ cup basic vanilla icing (page 33) or store-bought vanilla icing

1. Mix together the ingredients for making a vanilla cake (page 31). After the ingredients are fully combined, stir in the cinnamon, bananas, pineapple, and pecans.

2. Follow the instructions for baking the cake (page 31).

3. While the cake is cooling, prepare the icing (page 33) or open your store-bought icing.

4. After the cake has cooled, follow the cake ball method instructions (page 17). Note that this recipe calls for less icing than normal because the cake itself is already so rich and moist.

5. After the cake balls are dipped in white chocolate, place a piece of sugared or dried pineapple in the white chocolate cap.

FOR COATING AND DECORATING:

24 ounces white chocolate, for coating

About ½ cup sugared or dried pineapples, cut into small pieces, for garnish

Peanut Butter Banana

*We fondly refer to these cake balls as the King's Balls at The Cake Ball Company.
They are our ode to Elvis, and after you give 'em a taste, you won't be singing the blues!
The vanilla cake is baked with ripe bananas and creamy peanut butter. Mixing it with the cream
cheese icing really complements the flavors and creates a rich and creamy cake ball.*

1. Mix together the ingredients for making a vanilla cake (page 31). After the ingredients are fully combined, stir in the bananas and peanut butter.

2. Follow the instructions for baking the cake (page 31).

3. While the cake is cooling, prepare the icing (page 34) or open your store-bought icing.

4. After the cake has cooled, follow the cake ball method instructions (page 17).

5. After the cake balls are dipped in dark chocolate, place a dried banana chip in the dark chocolate cap.

Quick Tip: If you really dig peanut butter, like Elvis, try adding more to the recipe.

FOR THE CAKE AND ICING:

1 (18.25-ounce) box vanilla cake mix or basic vanilla cake (page 31)

3 ripe medium bananas, mashed (about 1½ cups)

⅓ cup creamy peanut butter

½ to ¾ cup basic cream cheese icing (page 34) or store-bought cream cheese icing

FOR COATING AND DECORATING:

24 ounces dark chocolate, for coating

About ½ cup dried banana chips, for garnish

Lemon

One summer, our kids had a lemonade stand and sold these cake balls with cups of lemonade. At the end of the day, they were sold out of cake balls but had plenty of lemonade left over! All of the proceeds went to help a local veterans' foundation. Maybe you can think of something similar to use these cake balls for good as well!

FOR THE CAKE AND ICING:

1 (18.25-ounce) box vanilla cake mix or basic vanilla cake (page 31)

Zest and juice from 2 large lemons

2½ tablespoons lemon extract

½ to ¾ cup basic vanilla icing (page 33) or store-bought vanilla icing

Zest from 1 large lemon

1. Mix together the ingredients for making a vanilla cake (page 31). After the ingredients are fully combined, stir in the lemon zest and juice, and lemon extract.

2. Follow the instructions for baking the cake (page 31).

3. While the cake is cooling, prepare the icing (page 33) or open your store-bought icing. Stir in the lemon zest with the icing before incorporating with the crumbled cake.

4. After the cake has cooled, follow the cake ball method instructions (page 17).

5. After the cake balls are dipped in white chocolate, drizzle them with fine lines. Sprinkle with the crushed lemon drops.

FOR COATING AND DECORATING:

24 ounces white chocolate, for coating

About ½ cup crushed lemon drop candies, for garnish

JINGLE BALLS

Jingle balls, jingle balls . . . cake balls all the way! Make the jolly old man the happiest he has ever been this Christmas. Leave him some cake balls with milk instead of cookies and milk! There are so many merry flavors to choose from, and we hear that Dark Chocolate Peppermint, Creamy Eggnog, and Gingerbread are his favorites. We don't want Santa to have all the fun, though. When you need a warm winter treat or a quick pick-me-up, Carrot Cake, Pumpkin Spice, and Cinnamon Streusel are an absolute perfect way to start any festive holiday morning.

Jingle Balls (from left to right):
Creamy Eggnog, Dark Chocolate Peppermint

Carrot Cake

Who would have thought that adding carrots (of all things!) to a sugary cake would be so delicious? Carrot cake tends to be more prevalent during the holidays, but we think it's great any time of year. If you don't like pecans, feel free to leave them out. This cake ball packs the hearty combination of pineapple, raisins, carrots, and spices—with a ton of flavor.

FOR THE CAKE AND ICING:

1 (18.25-ounce) box yellow cake mix or basic yellow cake (page 32)

3 teaspoons ground cinnamon

2 teaspoons vanilla extract

1 teaspoon freshly grated nutmeg

½ cup light brown sugar, packed

About 3 medium carrots, finely shredded (1½ cups)

1 cup raisins

1 cup canned crushed pineapple, drained

1 cup pecans, chopped finely

½ to ¾ cup basic cream cheese icing (page 34) or store-bought cream cheese icing

1. Mix together the ingredients for making a yellow cake (page 32). Stir in the cinnamon, vanilla, nutmeg, sugar, carrots, raisins, pineapple, and pecans.

2. Follow the instructions for baking the cake (page 32).

3. While the cake is cooling, prepare the icing (page 34) or open your store-bought icing.

4. After the cake has cooled, follow the cake ball method instructions (page 17).

5. After the cake balls are dipped in white chocolate, drizzle them with the chocolate and sprinkle with the raw sugar.

FOR COATING AND DECORATING:

24 ounces white chocolate, for coating

About ¼ cup raw sugar, for garnish

Dark Chocolate Peppermint

Robin's husband, who is a true chocolate and peppermint junkie, inspired this recipe. Our Chocolate Peppermint Cake Ball has gone through many changes over the years. We've made it with vanilla cake, we've tried different kinds of peppermint, and we've tried dipping it in white, dark, and milk chocolate. Ultimately, we decided that the recipe below is our favorite combination—and Robin's husband agrees!

1. Follow the instructions for baking a chocolate cake (page 30).

2. While the cake is cooling, prepare the icing (page 33) or open your store-bought icing.

3. After the cake has cooled, follow the cake ball method instructions (page 17). As you are stirring the icing with the cake crumbs, add the peppermint crunch.

4. After the cake balls are dipped in dark chocolate, drizzle them with fine lines. Do one at a time and sprinkle with peppermint crunch to give the cake balls a festive feel and a little more peppermint taste.

Quick Tip: *Try boxing up a few of these in festive holiday tins or boxes and give them to friends, family, or neighbors as gifts. They'll love you forever.*

FOR THE CAKE AND ICING:

1 (18.25-ounce) box chocolate cake mix or basic chocolate cake (page 30)

½ to ¾ cup basic chocolate icing (page 33) or store-bought chocolate icing

1 cup Andes Peppermint Crunch Baking Chips (look in the candy or baking aisle, or online)

FOR COATING AND DECORATING:

24 ounces dark chocolate, for coating

About ½ cup Andes Peppermint Crunch Baking Chips, for garnish (look in the candy or baking isle, or online)

Cinnamon Streusel

If you are invited to a holiday brunch this year, impress your friends and family with this tasty creation. A sweet streusel of pecans, brown sugar, and cinnamon laced throughout yellow cake is mixed with cream cheese icing to create a bite-size brunch treat that is easy to serve. Just set out the napkins and brunch away!

FOR THE CAKE AND ICING:

1 (18.25-ounce) box yellow cake mix or basic yellow cake (page 32)

4 ounces (1 stick) unsalted butter, melted

⅓ cup light brown sugar, packed

2 teaspoons ground cinnamon

½ cup finely chopped pecans

½ to ¾ cup basic cream cheese icing (page 34) or store-bought cream cheese icing

FOR COATING AND DECORATING:

24 ounces white chocolate, for coating

About ¼ cup ground cinnamon, for garnish

1. Mix together the ingredients for making a yellow cake (page 32). Add the butter and blend.

2. In a separate bowl, mix together the sugar, cinnamon, and pecans to create your streusel.

3. Pour half of the cake batter into the cake pan and sprinkle the streusel on top. Cover the streusel with the remaining cake batter.

4. Follow the instructions for baking the cake (page 32).

5. While the cake is cooling, prepare the icing (page 34) or open your store-bought icing.

6. After the cake has cooled, follow the cake ball method instructions (page 17).

7. After the cake balls are dipped in white chocolate, drizzle them with fine lines of chocolate and sprinkle with the cinnamon.

Gingerbread

It's beginning to look a lot like Christmas . . . or at least smell like it.
This is a Cake Ball Company favorite to bake, because rich aromas of
molasses and ginger fill the air when it's in the oven. Yum!

1. Mix together the ingredients for making a yellow cake (page 32). Add the sugar, molasses, ginger, and cinnamon.

2. Follow the instructions for baking the cake (page 32).

3. While the cake is cooling, prepare the icing (page 33) or open your store-bought icing.

4. After the cake has cooled, follow the cake ball method instructions (page 17).

5. After the cake balls are dipped in white chocolate, drizzle them with fine lines of chocolate and top with the gingersnaps.

Quick Tip: Traditionally, we decorate this cake ball with crushed gingersnaps, but the holiday decorating ideas are endless. Try capping them off with spicy cinnamon candies or candied orange peels.

FOR THE CAKE AND ICING:

1 (18.25-ounce) box yellow cake mix or basic yellow cake (page 32)

⅓ cup light brown sugar, packed

1 cup molasses

1 teaspoon ground ginger

1 teaspoon ground cinnamon

½ to ¾ cup basic vanilla icing (page 33) or store-bought vanilla icing

FOR COATING AND DECORATING:

24 ounces white chocolate, for coating

About ½ cup crushed gingersnap cookies, for garnish

Pumpkin Spice

Nothing says "fall" more than the appearance of pumpkins. But at The Cake Ball Company, nothing says "fall" more than the appearance of Pumpkin Spice Cake Balls! These cake balls are so incredible, you'll be longing for fall all year long. The yellow cake is baked with pumpkin puree and spices, then mixed with cream cheese icing and dunked in creamy white chocolate. Try making these, and see how many people you can get to fall for cake balls!

FOR THE CAKE AND ICING:

1 (18.25-ounce) box yellow cake mix or basic yellow cake (page 32)

1 (15-ounce) can pumpkin puree (not pumpkin pie mix)

⅔ cup light brown sugar, packed

2 teaspoons pumpkin pie spice

1 teaspoon ground cinnamon

½ to ¾ cup basic cream cheese icing (page 34) or store-bought cream cheese icing

1. Mix together the ingredients for making a yellow cake (page 32). Add the pumpkin puree, sugar, pumpkin pie spice, and cinnamon.

2. Follow the instructions for baking the cake (page 32).

3. While the cake is cooling, prepare the icing (page 34) or open your store-bought icing.

continues

Pumpkin Spice *continued*

FOR COATING AND DECORATING:

24 ounces white chocolate, for coating

About 55 pumpkin seeds, for garnish

4. After the cake has cooled, follow the cake ball method instructions (page 17).

5. After the cake balls are dipped in white chocolate, top each with a pumpkin seed.

Quick Tip: *At Halloween, try replacing the pumpkin seed with two sugared eyeballs. No one will be scared—they'll just be screaming for more!*

Creamy Eggnog

Eggnog sometimes gets a bad rap, but we love it. Charlotte's dad makes an amazing eggnog, so we thought that eggnog cake balls would be a fun way to celebrate his tasty concoction. If you can't make your own eggnog for this recipe, try to buy the fresh eggnog that is available around the holidays by the milk in grocery stores. Cheers!

FOR THE CAKE AND ICING:

- 1 (18.25-ounce) box yellow cake mix or basic yellow cake (page 32)
- 1 cup eggnog
- ¼ cup dark rum
- 1½ teaspoons freshly grated nutmeg
- ½ to ¾ cup basic vanilla icing (page 33) or store-bought vanilla icing

FOR COATING AND DECORATING:

- 24 ounces white chocolate, for coating
- About ¼ cup freshly grated nutmeg, for garnish

1. Mix together the ingredients for making a yellow cake, substituting the eggnog for the water, if using the box version, or for the milk, if making the cake from scratch (page 32). Stir in the rum and nutmeg.

2. Follow the instructions for baking the cake (page 32).

3. While the cake is cooling, prepare the icing (page 33) or open your store-bought icing.

4. After the cake has cooled, follow the cake ball method instructions (page 17).

5. After the cake balls are dipped in white chocolate, drizzle them with fine lines of chocolate and sprinkle with the nutmeg.

A LITTLE BIT TIPSY

Booze-spiked cake balls are our favorites to make. With bourbon, Champagne, and rum on hand, you could start your own little party while whipping up a batch of cake balls. The amount of liquor in the cake is fairly minimal, but it gives the cake a nice layer of flavor that will come through in the finished cake ball. So go ahead and roll a little, bake a little, dip a little, sip a little . . .

A Little Bit Tipsy (from left to right):
Almond Amaretto, Piña Colada, Irish Cream

Almond Amaretto

Amaretto is often added to desserts to enhance them with flavors of almond and apricot. These two perfect flavors also complement chocolate, so can't you imagine how delicious this cake ball is? Filled with amaretto, almond extract, and chopped almonds galore, it's nutty how good it is!

FOR THE CAKE AND ICING:

1 (18.25-ounce) box yellow cake mix or basic yellow cake (page 32)

¾ cup amaretto

1 (3.4-ounce) package instant vanilla pudding

½ teaspoon pure almond extract

½ cup chopped almonds

½ to ¾ cup basic vanilla icing (page 33) or store-bought vanilla icing

FOR COATING AND DECORATING:

24 ounces milk chocolate, for coating

About 55 slivered almonds, for garnish

1. Mix together the ingredients for making a yellow cake, reducing the water, if using the box version, or the milk, if making the cake from scratch, by ½ cup, and adding the amaretto (page 32). Stir in the vanilla pudding and almond extract.

2. Follow the instructions for baking the cake (page 32).

3. While the cake is cooling, prepare the icing (page 33) or open your store-bought icing.

4. After the cake has cooled, follow the cake ball method instructions (page 17). Add the almonds to the cake crumbles. Adding the almonds at this step gives the dough a nice crunchy texture.

5. After the cake balls are dipped in milk chocolate, top each with a slivered almond.

Raspberry Champagne

This cake ball is especially fun to make because it calls for Champagne. Once the top is popped on your Champagne, you will need to drink the rest while you bake the cake. You wouldn't want to be wasteful, right? We use a Blanc de Noir sparkling wine since the flavors tend to complement the raspberries. Enjoy!

1. Mix together the ingredients for making a vanilla cake, substituting the Champagne for the water, if using the box version, or for the milk, if making the cake from scratch (page 31). After the ingredients are fully combined, gently stir in the raspberries.

2. Follow the instructions for baking the cake (page 31).

3. While the cake is cooling, prepare the icing (page 34) or open your store-bought icing.

4. After the cake has cooled, follow the cake ball method instructions (page 17).

5. After the cake balls are dipped in white chocolate, place a raspberry in the white chocolate cap.

FOR THE CAKE AND ICING:

1 (18.25-ounce) box vanilla cake mix or basic vanilla cake (page 31)

1 cup Champagne or sparkling wine

1 pint fresh raspberries, rough chopped (about 2 cups)

½ to ¾ cup basic cream cheese icing (page 34) or store-bought cream cheese icing

FOR COATING AND DECORATING:

24 ounces white chocolate, for coating

About 55 raspberries, for garnish

Bourbon Pecan Pie

The great state of Tennessee was our inspiration for this cake ball. On a company trip to Nashville, we thought of this one while sampling some of Tennessee's finest. Our husbands prefer more bourbon than we call for in this recipe, so feel free to adjust the measurement slightly to suit your taste. I'm sure our husbands would probably like for it to come with bourbon on the rocks as a side dish as well.

1. Mix together the ingredients for making a yellow cake (page 32). After the ingredients are fully combined, stir in the bourbon, pecans, sugar, and light corn syrup.

2. Follow the instructions for baking the cake (page 32).

3. While the cake is cooling, prepare the icing (page 33) or open your store-bought icing.

4. After the cake has cooled, follow the cake ball method instructions (page 17).

5. After the cake balls are dipped in white chocolate, place a pecan in the white chocolate cap.

FOR THE CAKE AND ICING:

1 (18.25-ounce) box yellow cake mix or basic yellow cake (page 32)

½ cup bourbon

½ cup finely chopped pecans

½ cup light brown sugar, packed

¼ cup light corn syrup

½ to ¾ cup basic vanilla icing (page 33) or store-bought vanilla icing

FOR COATING AND DECORATING:

24 ounces white chocolate, for coating

About 55 pecans, for garnish

Irish Cream

This recipe was developed for a St. Patrick's Day party and has quickly become the house favorite. When we make it in our kitchen, it has to be rolled and put in the freezer immediately, so everyone doesn't eat it before it has a chance to reach its cake ball destiny. You'll agree that it has the luck o' the Irish!

FOR THE CAKE AND ICING:

- 1 (18.25-ounce) box yellow cake mix or basic yellow cake (page 32)
- ½ cup Irish cream liqueur
- ½ cup finely chopped pecans
- 1 (3.4-ounce) package instant vanilla pudding
- ½ to ¾ cup basic cream cheese icing (page 34) or store-bought cream cheese icing

1. Mix together the ingredients for making a yellow cake (page 32). After the ingredients are fully combined, stir in the Irish cream, pecans, and pudding.

2. Follow the instructions for baking the cake (page 32).

3. While the cake is cooling, prepare the icing (page 34) or open your store-bought icing.

continues

Irish Cream continued

FOR COATING AND DECORATING:

24 ounces milk chocolate, for coating

About ¼ cup clear sprinkles, for decoration

4. After the cake has cooled, follow the cake ball method instructions (page 17).

5. After the cake balls are dipped in milk chocolate, drizzle them with fine lines. Do one at a time and sprinkle with clear edible crystals to give each a shimmering sparkle.

Quick Tip: You can make these cake balls even more festive by decorating them with green sprinkles or shamrocks made of sugar. You could even try drizzling them with green candy melts, which are available in most craft stores.

Key West Rum Cake

Transport yourself to the tropics with this intoxicated cake ball. The yellow cake is baked with dark rum, pecans, and lime zest. Once the cake balls are dipped in white chocolate, your taste buds will set sail and take you to uncharted cake ball bliss.

1. Mix together the ingredients for making a yellow cake (page 32). Add the dark rum and vanilla pudding. After the ingredients are fully combined, stir in the pecans and lime zest.

2. Follow the instructions for baking the cake (page 32).

3. While the cake is cooling, prepare the icing (page 33) or open your store-bought icing.

4. After the cake has cooled, follow the cake ball method instructions (page 17).

5. After the cake balls are dipped in white chocolate, top each with a little lime zest.

FOR THE CAKE AND ICING:

1 (18.25-ounce) box yellow cake mix or basic yellow cake (page 32)

½ cup dark rum

1 (3.4-ounce) package instant vanilla pudding

1 cup finely chopped pecans

Zest from 1 large lime

½ to ¾ cup basic vanilla icing (page 33) or store-bought vanilla icing

FOR COATING AND DECORATING:

24 ounces white chocolate, for coating

Zest from 1 large lime, for garnish

Margarita Lime

This recipe came to us one night at a fun happy hour. We don't think there's anything better than a well-made margarita. Well, maybe besides this cake ball—which won't give you a hangover! This is Robin's favorite cake ball just for that reason. The salty/sweet garnish makes this cake ball pretty addictive, so beware!

1. Mix together the ingredients for making a vanilla cake (page 31). After the ingredients are fully combined, stir in the lime puree, orange liqueur, and sea salt.

2. Follow the instructions for baking the cake (page 31).

3. While the cake is cooling, prepare the icing (page 34) or open your store-bought icing.

4. After the cake has cooled, follow the cake ball method instructions (page 17).

FOR THE CAKE AND ICING:

1 (18.25-ounce) box vanilla cake mix or basic vanilla cake (page 31)

½ cup lime puree (see Quick Tip)

½ cup orange liqueur

½ teaspoon fine sea salt

½ to ¾ cup basic cream cheese icing (page 34) or store-bought cream cheese icing

continues

Margarita Lime *continued*

FOR COATING AND DECORATING:

24 ounces white chocolate, for coating

5 tablespoons lime sugar, for garnish (see Quick Tip)

2 tablespoons fine sea salt, for garnish

5. After the cake balls are dipped in white chocolate, you can decorate. In a small bowl, combine the lime sugar and sea salt. Dip a spoon in the melted white chocolate and drizzle fine lines across each cake ball. Do one at a time and sprinkle with the lime sugar mixture after each drizzling.

Quick Tip: You can buy lime puree at most specialty food stores or online. We really like The Perfect Puree of Napa Valley®. We garnish these cake balls with a mixture of lime sugar and sea salt. We buy the lime sugar from Whole Foods, but you can make your own by combining ½ cup of chopped lime zest and 1½ cups of sugar in a food processor.

Piña Colada

You just can't beat a great piña colada on the beach, but in Dallas, we don't get the chance to visit the beach often. This cake ball was created to at least let our taste buds get away. Yellow cake is baked with dark rum, crushed pineapple, and cream of coconut to create one scrumptious, beach-worthy cake ball.

1. Mix together the ingredients for making a yellow cake (page 32). After the ingredients are fully combined, stir in the dark rum, pineapple, and cream of coconut.

2. Follow the instructions for baking the cake (page 32).

3. While the cake is cooling, prepare the icing (page 34) or open your store-bought icing.

4. After the cake has cooled, follow the cake ball method instructions (page 17).

5. After the cake balls are dipped in white chocolate, place a piece of shaved coconut in the white chocolate cap.

FOR THE CAKE AND ICING:

1 (18.25-ounce) box yellow cake mix or basic yellow cake (page 32)

½ cup dark rum

¼ cup canned crushed pineapple, drained

¼ cup cream of coconut (not coconut milk)

½ to ¾ cup basic cream cheese icing (page 34) or store-bought cream cheese icing

FOR COATING AND DECORATING:

24 ounces white chocolate, for coating

About ½ cup sweetened shaved coconut, for garnish

Tiramisu

Tiramisu means "pick-me-up" in Italian, with a nod to the sugar and coffee it includes. As we all know, caffeine and sugar never fail to pick us up, and this cake ball will surely lift your spirits, too. The yellow cake is baked with coffee granules and brandy, then blended with cream cheese icing. After it takes a dunk in milk chocolate, crushed ladyfingers finish off your new favorite pick-me-up!

FOR THE CAKE AND ICING:

1 (18.25-ounce) box yellow cake mix or basic yellow cake (page 32)

4 teaspoons instant coffee granules

¼ cup brandy

½ to ¾ cup basic cream cheese icing (page 34) or store-bought cream cheese icing

FOR COATING AND DECORATING:

24 ounces dark chocolate, for coating

About ½ cup melted milk chocolate, for decoration

About ½ cup crushed ladyfinger biscuits, for garnish (about 10)

1. Mix together the ingredients for making a yellow cake (page 32). Stir in the instant coffee granules and brandy.

2. Follow the instructions for baking the cake (page 32).

3. While the cake is cooling, prepare the icing (page 34) or open your store-bought icing.

4. After the cake has cooled, follow the cake ball method instructions (page 17).

5. After the cake balls are dipped in dark chocolate, drizzle them with the melted milk chocolate and sprinkle with the crushed ladyfingers.

FUN WITH CAKE BALLS

Okay, so all cake balls are equally fun to make, of course, but this chapter focuses on some really spectacular flavors that take the cake! Chocolate Malted Milk Cake Balls are made with Whoppers. Cookies and Cream Cake Balls have nice chunks of Oreo cookies crumbled in. S'mores Cake Balls are a sweet combo of graham cracker cake blended with chocolate chips and marshmallows. Transport yourself back to your carefree childhood, forget your worries, and have a blast with these recipes.

Fun With Cake Balls (from left to right):
Cookies and Cream, Snickerdoodle, S'mores

Chocolate Malted Milk

We are starting this chapter with a flavor inspired by our favorite old-fashioned soda fountain and its yummy malts. This one starts with delicious vanilla cake baked with malted milk. It is then blended with vanilla icing and chopped Whopper candies. How great is that?

FOR THE CAKE AND ICING:

1 (18.25-ounce) box vanilla cake mix or basic vanilla cake (page 31)

¾ cup malted milk powder

½ to ¾ cup basic vanilla icing (page 33) or store-bought vanilla icing

2 (5-ounce) boxes Whoppers, chopped

FOR COATING AND DECORATING:

24 ounces dark chocolate, for coating

About ½ cup melted milk chocolate, for decoration

1. Mix together the ingredients for making a vanilla cake (page 31). Stir in the malted milk powder.

2. Follow the instructions for baking the cake (page 31).

3. While the cake is cooling, prepare the icing (page 33) or open your store-bought icing.

4. After the cake has cooled, follow the cake ball method instructions (page 17). Add the Whoppers to the cake crumbles and icing. Adding the Whoppers at this step gives the dough a nice crunchy texture. Be sure to remove any large pieces of candy.

5. After the cake balls are dipped in dark chocolate, drizzle them with the melted milk chocolate.

Quick Tip: *For even more malted milk flavor and crunch, you can try chopping more Whoppers roughly and sprinkling them over the top of each cake ball after dipping the balls in the dark chocolate.*

Honey Granola

While researching some fun new recipe ideas, we wanted something that would add crunch and texture to our decadently doughy cake balls. Someone suggested granola, and this new recipe was born. This hippie cake ball paired with hot coffee is morning-time nirvana.

FOR THE CAKE AND ICING:

1 (18.25-ounce) box yellow cake mix or basic yellow cake (page 32)

2 cups honey-flavored granola, divided

½ to ¾ cup basic vanilla icing (page 33) or store-bought vanilla icing

FOR COATING AND DECORATING:

24 ounces dark chocolate, for coating

About ½ cup honey-flavored granola, for garnish

1. Mix together the ingredients for making a yellow cake (page 32). After the ingredients are fully combined, add 1 cup of the honey granola.

2. Follow the instructions for baking the cake (page 32).

3. While the cake is cooling, prepare the icing (page 33) or open your store-bought icing.

4. After the cake has cooled, follow the cake ball method instructions (page 17). Add the additional 1 cup of honey granola to the cake crumbles. Adding the granola at this step gives the dough a nice crunchy texture.

5. After the cake balls are dipped in dark chocolate, drizzle them with the chocolate and top with more honey granola.

Quick Tip: *You can also try adding actual honey to the cake batter before baking, for a bolder honey taste.*

Chai Latte

Transport yourself to the East with a chai latte cake ball. A chai latte is a creamy delicious tea that is brewed with Indian spices. Adding prepared chai tea to vanilla cake re-creates this yummy beverage in cake ball form. We hope you'll love it as much as we do.

1. Mix together the ingredients for making a vanilla cake, substituting the chai tea liquid for the water, if using the box version, or for the milk, if making the cake from scratch (page 31).

2. Follow the instructions for baking the cake (page 31).

3. While the cake is cooling, prepare the icing (page 33) or open your store-bought icing.

4. After the cake has cooled, follow the cake ball method instructions (page 17).

5. After the cake balls are dipped in white chocolate, drizzle them with the chocolate and sprinkle with the chai tea powder.

FOR THE CAKE AND ICING:

1 (18.25-ounce) box vanilla cake mix or basic vanilla cake (page 31)

1⅓ cups prepared chai tea

½ to ¾ cup basic vanilla icing (page 33) or store-bought vanilla icing

FOR COATING AND DECORATING:

24 ounces white chocolate, for coating

About ¼ cup chai tea powder, for garnish

Quick Tip: *If you have trouble finding the chai tea powder, you can garnish the cake balls with a mixture of cardamom, ginger, cloves, and cinnamon. These are the basic flavors of a chai latte.*

Dreamsicle

*We both have fond memories of enjoying orange-flavored push pops during the
sweltering hot Texas summers. You always had to eat them super fast before you had
sticky orange sweetness dripping down your arms. These cake balls might not be
all natural or remotely healthy, but at least they won't drip orange goo down your
arms when you eat them—and they sure taste pretty good, too.*

1. Mix together the ingredients for making a vanilla cake, substituting the orange soda for the water, if using the box version, or for the milk, if making the cake from scratch (page 31). After the ingredients are fully combined, stir in the orange gelatin.

2. Follow the instructions for baking the cake (page 31).

3. While the cake is cooling, prepare the icing (page 33) or open your store-bought icing.

4. After the cake has cooled, follow the cake ball method instructions (page 17).

5. After the cake balls are dipped in white chocolate, sprinkle them with the sugar crystals or place a gummy sugared orange slice in the white chocolate cap.

FOR THE CAKE AND ICING:

1 (18.25-ounce) box vanilla cake mix or basic vanilla cake (page 31)

1 cup orange soda

1 (6-ounce) package orange-flavored gelatin

½ to ¾ cup basic vanilla icing (page 33) or store-bought vanilla icing

FOR THE COATING AND DECORATING:

24 ounces white chocolate, for coating

About ½ cup orange sugar crystals (or 55 gummy sugared orange slices), for garnish

Oatmeal Raisin Cookie Dough

One of our favorite things about cake balls is the fact that they inherently have the consistency of cookie dough, and you get to eat as much dough as you want without the fear of raw eggs. In this recipe, eating these cake balls is exactly like eating oatmeal raisin cookie dough dipped in creamy white chocolate. Mmm.

FOR THE CAKE AND ICING:

1 (18.25-ounce) box vanilla cake mix or basic vanilla cake (page 31)

½ cup light brown sugar, packed

2 teaspoons ground cinnamon

2 cups quick-cooking oats

1 cup small raisins

½ to ¾ cup basic vanilla icing (page 33) or store-bought vanilla icing

FOR COATING AND DECORATING:

24 ounces white chocolate, for coating

About 55 small raisins, for garnish

About ½ cup brown sugar crystals, for garnish

1. Mix together the ingredients for making a vanilla cake (page 31). After the ingredients are fully combined, stir in the sugar, cinnamon, oats, and raisins.

2. Follow the instructions for baking the cake (page 31).

3. While the cake is cooling, prepare the icing (page 33) or open your store-bought icing.

4. After the cake has cooled, follow the cake ball method instructions (page 17).

5. After the cake balls are dipped in white chocolate, place a raisin in the white chocolate cap and garnish with the sugar crystals.

Cookies and Cream

What if we told you that it was possible to eat moist vanilla cake, crunchy chocolaty Oreos, rich cream cheese icing, and decadent milk chocolate all in one bite? Would you believe us? Well, we're here to tell you it is definitely possible. Give this recipe a whirl, but try not to pass out from the sugar intoxication.

1. Mix together the ingredients for making a vanilla cake (page 31). After the ingredients are fully combined, stir in 1 cup of the chopped Oreos.

2. Follow the instructions for baking the cake (page 31).

3. While the cake is cooling, prepare the icing (page 34) or open your store-bought icing.

4. After the cake has cooled, follow the cake ball method instructions (page 17). As you incorporate the icing with the crumbled cake, add the second cup of crushed Oreos.

5. After the cake balls are dipped in milk chocolate, drizzle them with the chocolate and top with the crushed Oreos.

FOR THE CAKE AND ICING:

1 (18.25-ounce) box vanilla cake mix or basic vanilla cake (page 31)

2 cups coarsely chopped Oreos, divided (about 25)

½ to ¾ cup basic cream cheese icing (page 34) or store-bought cream cheese icing

FOR COATING AND DECORATING:

24 ounces milk chocolate, for coating

About ½ cup crushed Oreos, for garnish (about 10)

Salted Peanut Butter

Forget the jelly! We think nothing goes better with peanut butter than chocolate. And, the sprinkling of sea salt gives this cake ball that unbelievable salty/sweet combination that is just soooooo good.

FOR THE CAKE AND ICING:

1 (18.25-ounce) box vanilla cake mix or basic vanilla cake (page 31)

½ cup creamy peanut butter

½ to ¾ cup basic vanilla icing (page 33) or store-bought vanilla icing

FOR COATING AND DECORATING:

24 ounces milk chocolate, for coating

About 55 salted peanuts, for garnish

Fine sea salt, for garnish

1. Mix together the ingredients for making a vanilla cake (page 31). After the ingredients are fully combined, stir in the peanut butter.

2. Follow the instructions for baking the cake (page 31).

3. While the cake is cooling, prepare the icing (page 33) or open your store-bought icing.

4. After the cake has cooled, follow the cake ball method instructions (page 17).

5. After the cake balls are dipped in milk chocolate, place a peanut in the milk chocolate cap. Sprinkle with the sea salt.

S'mores

Who doesn't love s'mores at a cookout? This cake ball was inspired by our kids, who love a good camping trip, if only because they get to make s'mores. In this cake ball, vanilla cake is baked with crumbled graham crackers and mixed with cream cheese icing, chocolate chips, and marshmallows—all of the flavors that make s'mores so darn good.

FOR THE CAKE AND ICING:

- 1 (18.25-ounce) box vanilla cake mix or basic vanilla cake (page 31)
- 1 cup finely crumbled graham crackers (about 14)
- ½ to ¾ cup basic cream cheese icing (page 34) or store-bought cream cheese icing
- ¾ cup mini marshmallows, cut into tiny pieces
- ½ cup mini chocolate chips

1. Mix together the ingredients for making a vanilla cake (page 31). After the ingredients are fully combined, stir in the graham cracker crumbles.

2. Follow the instructions for baking the cake (page 31).

3. While the cake is cooling, prepare the icing (page 34) or open your store-bought icing.

4. After the cake has cooled, follow the cake ball method instructions (page 17). As you are stirring the icing with the cake crumbs, add the mini marshmallows and mini chocolate chips.

5. After the cake balls are dipped in dark chocolate, place half a mini marshmallow in the dark chocolate cap. Drizzle the cake balls one at a time with the dark chocolate and sprinkle with the graham cracker crumbs.

Quick Tip: Cutting the marshmallows into tiny pieces will keep the cake balls from getting too lumpy, so try to cut them as small as you can.

FOR COATING AND DECORATING:

24 ounces dark chocolate, for coating

About ½ cup mini marshmallows, cut in half, for garnish

About ¼ cup graham cracker crumbs, for garnish

Salted Caramel

When we attended a food show a few years ago, salted caramels were all the rage.
So, we just had to make a cake ball from this salty and sweet combination.
This recipe is quite different than the way we make them at The Cake Ball Company,
but we wanted to keep it short and simple for you. But don't worry: you'll get the same
flavor effect of caramel, sugar, chocolate, and salty goodness. That's a promise.

1. Mix together the ingredients for making a vanilla cake, reducing the water, if using the box version, or the milk, if making the cake from scratch, by ½ cup (page 31). After the ingredients are fully combined, stir in the caramel sundae syrup and sea salt.

2. Follow the instructions for baking the cake (page 31).

3. While the cake is cooling, prepare the icing (page 34) or open your store-bought icing.

4. After the cake has cooled, follow the cake ball method instructions (page 17).

5. After the cake balls are dipped in dark chocolate, drizzle them with the chocolate and sprinkle with the sea salt.

Quick Tip: *You can also try topping these with a piece of caramel candy cut in half and then sprinkling with sea salt.*

FOR THE CAKE AND ICING:

1 (18.25-ounce) box vanilla cake mix or basic vanilla cake (page 31)

1 (20-ounce) jar or bottle of caramel sundae syrup

1 teaspoon fine sea salt

½ to ¾ cup basic cream cheese icing (page 34) or store-bought cream cheese icing

FOR COATING AND DECORATING:

24 ounces dark chocolate, for coating

About ¼ cup fine sea salt, for garnish

Snickerdoodle

We haven't figured out what's more fun: making these delicious cake balls or just saying "snickerdoodle." This cake ball with the silly name is so tasty because it has crumbled cookies in the dough. The lively sugar cookie and cinnamon taste will definitely win you over.

FOR THE CAKE AND ICING:

1 (18.25-ounce) box yellow cake mix or basic yellow cake (page 32)

2 teaspoons ground cinnamon

½ to ¾ cup basic cream cheese icing (page 34) or store-bought cream cheese icing

6 large snickerdoodle cookies, crumbled

FOR COATING AND DECORATING:

24 ounces white chocolate, for coating

About ¼ cup ground cinnamon and granulated sugar, for garnish

1. Mix together the ingredients for making a yellow cake (page 32). Stir in the cinnamon.

2. Follow the instructions for baking the cake (page 32).

3. While the cake is cooling, prepare the icing (page 34) or open your store-bought icing.

4. After the cake has cooled, follow the cake ball method instructions (page 17). Add the crumbled snickerdoodle cookies to the cake crumbles.

5. After the cake balls are dipped in white chocolate, drizzle them with the chocolate and top with the cinnamon and sugar.

Quick Tip: *You can make your own snickerdoodle cookies for this recipe, or save yourself the hassle and just buy them. The crunchier the cookie, the better! You can also try topping the cake balls with a piece of a snickerdoodle cookie instead of sprinkling with cinnamon and sugar.*

Tres Leches

*Tres leches is a popular Mexican cake that is soaked in three types of milk,
hence the name. In our version, we use yellow cake that is soaked in whole milk,
condensed milk, and heavy cream. Low fat? No. Crazy good? Yes! The cake
is so moist that you don't even need to add icing. In fact, we always pick at this cake
right out of the pan so much that there is hardly any left to roll into balls!*

1. Follow the instructions for baking a yellow cake (page 32).

2. While the cake is cooling, mix together the whole milk, condensed milk, and heavy cream. Poke holes on top of the cake with the end of a spoon and pour the milk mixture over the warm cake. Place the cake in the refrigerator for at least 3 hours.

4. Once the milks are fully absorbed into the cake, follow the cake ball method instructions (page 17). As you won't be using icing in this recipe, skip that part!

5. After the cake balls are dipped in white chocolate, top with a bit of sweetened condensed milk.

FOR THE CAKE AND ICING:

1 (18.25-ounce) box yellow cake mix or basic yellow cake (page 32)

¼ cup whole milk

1 (14-ounce) can sweetened condensed milk

¼ cup heavy whipping cream

FOR COATING AND DECORATING:

24 ounces white chocolate, for coating

About ½ cup sweetened condensed milk, for garnish

Formulas for Metric Conversion

Ounces to grams   multiply ounces by 28.35
Pounds to grams   multiply pounds by 453.5

Cups to liters   multiply cups by .24
Fahrenheit to Centigrade   subtract 32 from Fahrenheit, multiply by 5 and divide by 9

Metric Equivalents for Volume

U.S.	Metric
⅛ tsp.	0.6 ml
¼ tsp.	1.2 ml
½ tsp.	2.5 ml
¾ tsp.	3.7 ml
1 tsp.	5 ml
1½ tsp.	7.4 ml
2 tsp.	10 ml
1 Tbsp.	15 ml
1½ Tbsp.	22.0 ml
2 Tbsp. (⅛ cup/1 fl. oz)	30 ml
3 Tbsp.	45 ml
¼ cup (2 fl. oz)	59 ml
⅓ cup	79 ml
½ cup (4 fl. oz)	118 ml
⅔ cup	158 ml
¾ cup (6 fl. oz)	178 ml
1 cup (8 fl. oz)	237 ml
1¼ cups	300 ml
1½ cups	355 ml
1¾ cups	425 ml
2 cups (1 pint/16 fl. oz)	500 ml
3 cups	725 ml
1 quart (32 fl. oz)	.95 liters
1 gallon (128 fl. oz)	3.8 liters

Oven Temperatures

Degrees Fahrenheit	Degrees Centigrade	British Gas Marks
200°	93°	—
250°	120°	½
275°	140°	1
300°	150°	2
325°	165°	3
350°	175°	4
375°	190°	5
400°	200°	6
450°	230°	8

Metric Equivalents for Weight

U.S.	Metric
1 oz	28 g
2 oz	57 g
3 oz	85 g
4 oz	113 g
5 oz	142 g
6 oz	170 g
7 oz	198 g
8 oz	227 g
16 oz (1 lb.)	454 g
2.2 lbs.	1 kilogram

Metric Equivalents for Butter

U.S.	Metric
2 tsp.	10 g
1 Tbsp.	15 g
1½ Tbsp.	22.5 g
2 Tbsp. (1 oz)	27 g
3 Tbsp.	42 g
4 Tbsp.	56 g
4 oz. (1 stick)	110 g
8 oz. (2 sticks)	220 g

Metric Equivalents for Length

U.S.	Metric
¼ inch	.65 cm
½ inch	1.25 cm
1 inch	2.50 cm
2 inches	5.00 cm
3 inches	6.00 cm
4 inches	8.00 cm
5 inches	11.00 cm
6 inches	15.00 cm
7 inches	18.00 cm
8 inches	20.00 cm
9 inches	23.00 cm
12 inches	30.50 cm
15 inches	38.00 cm

Source: Herbst, Sharon Tyler. *The Food Lover's Companion.* 3rd ed. Hauppauge: Barron's, 2001.

Acknowledgments

Wow! What an amazing experience it was to write this cookbook. From the moment Holly with Hollan Publishing called and asked us to consider writing this book, to seeing our hard work come to life in the pages of *Cake Balls*, the journey has been a blast.

Our customers often ask for tips on making yummy cake balls, so we couldn't let the opportunity slip by to get everything in print. And, as The Original Cake Ball Company, we wanted to say thank you to our loyal cake ball fans for supporting us through the years. What better way to do that than to offer all of our tips and tricks in a book? We hope you all have hours of fun recreating our tasty treats.

Although there are many people who were essential in helping us to write this book, we would first like to thank our wonderful husbands, Jeff and Erich. They spent many hours looking after our precious kids, while we got creative in the kitchen and then ran to our computers to get it all down. Their undying support is what keeps us going, and we appreciate them more than they will ever know.

We would especially like to thank our children, Jackson, Luke, Elizabeth and Morgan for being sweet and patient kiddos while we have been chasing our dreams over the past six years. We also hope that they are inspired by our dedication and know that their dreams can be realized too if they work hard, stay focused and remain positive.

Our parents are an important ingredient in the *Cake Balls* mix too. Bobby, Cheryl, Bob, and Betsy, y'all are priceless. We hope this book finds you relaxing in a hammock somewhere breezy eating cake balls. An extra special thank you to Gammy Ball (Cheryl) for teaching Robin how to make cake balls years ago and supporting this growing craze over the years. Without you, Gams, there would be no Cake Ball Company.

And, we have to say thank you to all of our friends and CBC family (employees) who have helped to spread the cake ball love across the nation. Our business has grown by word-of-mouth over the years, and the undying support you have given us has helped to make that happen. We love and appreciate each and every one of you and owe you all a big glass of Chardonnay! (Oh, we should probably thank the grapes that make Chardonnay too, as it often helps us to get through the more insane times at work.)

Finally, we need to thank Holly and Alan at Hollan Publishing whose phone call got this ball rolling. And, also Jordana and Kärstin at Running Press. Y'all have done a fantastic job holding the hands of two somewhat crazy girls who have never authored a book before. We appreciate all of your patience and help.

Index